Cancer
2001

Teri King's Astrological Horoscopes for 2001

Cancer

Teri King's complete horoscope
for all those whose birthdays fall between
21 June and 22 July

Teri King

ELEMENT

Shaftesbury, Dorset • Boston, Massachusetts
Melbourne, Victoria

© Element Books Limited 2000
Text © Teri King 2000

First published in Great Britain in 2000 by
Element Books Limited
Shaftesbury, Dorset SP7 8BP

Published in the USA in 2000 by
Element Books, Inc.
160 North Washington Street, Boston, MA 02114

Published in Australia in 2000 by
Element Books
and distributed by Penguin Australia Limited
487 Maroondah Highway, Ringwood, Victoria 3134

Cover design and illustration by Slatter-Anderson
Design by Mark Slader
Typeset by The Bridgewater Book Company
Printed and bound in Great Britain by
Omnia Books Limited, Glasgow

British Library Cataloguing in Publication
data available

Library of Congress Cataloging in Publication
data available

ISBN 1 86204 781 2

Element Books regrets that it cannot enter into any correspondence
with readers requesting information about their horoscopes.

Contents

Cancer

21 June – 22 July

Ruling Planet: **The Moon**

Element: **Water**

Quality: **Feminine**

Planetary Principle: **Love**

Primal Desire: **Security**

Colour: **Violet**

Jewels: **Emerald**

Day: **Monday**

Magical Number: **2**

Famous Cancer
**Ernest Hemingway, Dalai Lama, Degas,
Louis Armstrong, Rembrandt, Marcel Proust,
John D Rockefeller, Harrison Ford,
Princess Diana, Paul Rubens.**

Introduction

ASTROLOGY HAS MANY USES, not least of which is its ability to help us to understand both ourselves and other people. Unfortunately there are many misconceptions and confusions associated with it, such as that old chestnut – how can a zodiac forecast be accurate for all the millions of people born under one particular sign?

The answer to this is that all horoscopes published in newspapers, books and magazines are, of necessity, of a general nature. Unless an astrologer can work from the date, time and place of your birth, the reading given will only be true for the typical member of your sign.

For instance, let's take a person born on 9 August. This person is principally a subject of Leo, simply because the Sun occupied that section of the heavens known as Leo between 23 July and 22 August. However, when delving into astrology at its most serious, there are other influences which need to be taken into consideration – for example, the Moon. This planet enters a fresh sign every 48 hours. On the birth date in question it may have been in, say, Virgo. And if this were the case it would make our particular subject both Leo (Sun representing willpower) and Virgo (Moon representing instincts) or, if you will, a Leo/Virgo. Then again the rising sign of 'ascendant' must also be taken into consideration. This also changes constantly as the Earth revolves: approximately every two hours a new section of the heavens comes into view and a new sign passes over the horizon. The rising sign is of the utmost importance, determining the image projected by the subject to the outside world – in effect, the personality.

The time of birth is essential when compiling a birth chart. Let us suppose that in this particular instance Leo was rising at the time of birth. Now, because two of the three main influences are Leo, our sample case would be fairly typical of his or her sign, possessing all the faults and attributes associated with it. However, if the Moon and ascendant had been in Virgo, then, whilst our subject would certainly display some of the Leo attributes or faults, it is more than likely that for the most part he or she would feel and behave more like a Virgoan.

As if life weren't complicated enough, this procedure must be carried through to take into account all the remaining planets. The position and signs of Mercury, Venus, Mars, Jupiter, Saturn, Uranus, Neptune and Pluto must all be discovered, plus the aspect formed from one planet to another. The calculation and interpretation of these movements by an astrologer will then produce an individual birth chart.

Because the heavens are constantly changing, it is very rare for two people to have identical charts. Although it is not inconceivable that it could happen, this would mean that the two subjects were born not only on the same date and at the same time, but also in the same place. Should such an incident occur, then the deciding factors as to how these individuals would differ in their approach to life, love, career, financial prospects and so on would be due to environmental and parental influence.

Returning to our hypothetical Leo: our example with the rising Sun in Leo and Moon in Virgo may find it useful not only to read up on his or her Sun sign (Leo) but also to read the section dealing with Virgo (the Moon). Nevertheless, this does not invalidate Sun sign astrology. This is because of the great power the Sun possesses: in any chart the Sun plays an important role.

Belief in astrology does not necessarily mean believing in totally determined lives, that our actions are predestined and we have no control over our fate. What it does clearly show is that our lives run in cycles, for both good and bad and, with the aid of astrology, we can make the most of, or minimize, certain patterns and tendencies. How this is done is entirely up to the individual. For example, if you are in possession of the knowledge that you are about to experience a lucky few days or weeks, then you can make the most of them by pushing ahead with plans. You can also be better prepared for illness, misfortune, romantic upset and every adversity.

Astrology should be used as it was originally intended – as a guide, especially to character. In this direction it is invaluable and it can help us in all aspects of friendship, work and romance. It makes it easier for us to see ourselves as we really are and, what's more, as others see us. We can recognize both our own weaknesses and strengths and those of others. It can give us both outer confidence and inner peace.

In the following pages you will find personality profiles and an in-depth look at the year ahead from all possible angles including numerology, Monthly and Daily Guides, and your Sun sign partner.

Used wisely, astrology can help you through life. It is not intended to encourage complacency, since, in the final analysis, what you do with your life is up to you. This book will aid you in adopting the correct attitude to the year ahead and thus maximize your chances of success. Positive thinking is encouraged because this helps us to attract positive situations. Allow astrology to walk hand in hand with you and you will be increasing your chances of success and happiness.

How Does Astrology Work?

YOU OFTEN HEAR PEOPLE say that there is no scientific explanation for astrology. However, astrological calculations may be explained in a very precise way, and they can be done by anyone with a little practice and a knowledge of the movement of stars and planets. It is the interpretations and conclusions drawn from these observations that are not necessarily consistent or verifiable, and, to be sure, predicted events do not always happen. Yet astrology has lasted in our culture for over 3,000 years, so there must be something in it!

So how can we explain astrology? Well, each individual birth sign has its own set of deep-seated characteristics, and an understanding of these can give you fresh insights into why you behave as you do. Reading an astrological interpretation, even if it is just to find out how, say, a new relationship might develop, will make you think about yourself in a very deep way. But it is important to remember that the stars don't determine your fate; it is up to you to use them to the best advantage in any situation.

Although astrology, like many other 'alternative' practices such as homeopathy, dowsing and telepathy, cannot be explained completely, there have been convincing experiments that have shown that it works far more often than chance would allow. The best-known studies are those of the French statistician, Michel Gauquelin, whose results were checked by a professor at the University of London who declared, grudgingly, that 'there was something in it'.

An important aspect of astrology is that it looks at how the Sun and the Moon affect the natural world around us every day. For instance, the rise and fall of the tides is purely a result of the movement and position of the Moon and Sun relative to the Earth. If this massive gravitational pull can move the oceans of the Earth, what does it do to us? After all, we are, on average, over 60 per cent water!

When it comes to the ways in which the Sun influences the world, a whole book could be written about on the subject. The influences we know about include day length, heat, light, solar storms, as well as magnetic, ultra-violet and many other forms of radiation. And all this from over 90 million miles away! For example, observation of birds has shown that before migration – which is governed by changes in the length of days – birds put on extra layers of fat, and also that they experience nocturnal restlessness shortly before setting off on their travels. I'm not suggesting that we put on weight and experience sleepless nights because of the time of year, but many people will tell you that different seasons affect them in different ways. Another example from the natural world is a curious species of giant worm which lives in underground caverns in the South Pacific. Twice a year, as the Sun is rising and the tide is at its highest, these worms come to the surface of the ocean. The inhabitants of the islands consider them a great delicacy. There are so many examples of how Earth's creatures respond to the influences of the Moon and the Sun that it is only common sense to wonder whether the position of other planets also has an effect, even if it is more subtle and less easy to identify.

Finally, we come to the question of how astrology might work in predicting future events. As we have seen, the planetary bodies are likely to affect us in all sorts of ways, both physically and mentally. Most often, subtle changes in the positions of the planets will influence our emotional states and, of course, this will affect how we behave. By drawing up a chart based on precise birth times, and by using their intuition, some astrologers can make precise predictions about how planetary influences in the years ahead are likely to shape the life of an individual. Many people are very surprised at how well an astrologer seems to 'understand' them after reading a commentary on their birth chart.

Stranger still are the astrologers who appear to be able to predict future events many years before they happen. The most famous example of all is the 16th-century French astrologer, Nostradamus, who is well known for having predicted the possibility of world destruction at the end of this millennium. Don't worry, I think I can cheerfully put everyone's mind at rest by assuring you that the world will go on for a good many years yet. Although Nostradamus certainly made some very accurate predictions in his lifetime, his prophecies for our future are very obscure and are hotly disputed by all the experts. Mind you, it is quite clear that there are likely to be massive changes ahead. It is a possibility, for instance, that information may come to light about past civilizations which are now sunk under the Mediterranean Sea: this will give us a good idea about how people lived in the past, and provide pointers as to how we should live in the future. Try not to fear, dear reader. Astrology is a tool for us to use, and if we use it wisely, no doubt we will survive with greater wisdom and a greater respect for our world and for each other.

The Sun In Cancer

YOU'RE A CHILD OF THE MOON, and you wear your moods on your sleeve, along with a lot of longing. You are the original creature of desire and have more cravings than you or anybody else knows what to do with. You're the kind of person who everyone needs to know and experience. You have a way of anticipating someone's needs before they happen, and of offering your services before anyone has had the chance to ask.

Because of your supersensitive emotional approach to others, you're a lot more vulnerable than the average person. Be careful where you place your sympathies, as people may take your generous nature for granted and tread on you when you least expect it. Such an experience is cause for an instant retreat to scrutinize your bruised and swollen sensitivities. It's very difficult for you to detach yourself from offensive behaviour aimed in your direction and to chalk it up to someone's acid indigestion or a bad day at the office.

Others need to remember that you mean well, because everything that you do is in someone's best interest. When it comes to your own interests, you crave constant reassurance that you are loved, needed, wanted and appreciated, and that your presence produces pleasure. When you let yourself relax and enjoy your life, you have a wondrous way of making everything seem better.

In general, you're a romantic who cries at weddings, weeps over memorable moments and sniffles at sentimental movies. The problems in your own life often assume the proportions of those on stage and screen. You spend a great deal of time trying to define yourself through other people. Likewise, you allocate to others far more power than you ever allow yourself.

The Year Ahead: Overview

DURING THE YEAR 2001, that slow-moving planet, Pluto, is crawling through the fiery sign of Sagittarius. This area of your chart is devoted to health and to your everyday work. Because of Pluto's disruptive influence, you can't expect everything to run smoothly in these departments. For example, workmates may be deliberately obstructive; however, instead of running off into a corner and beginning to sob, it might be a good idea to find out what is motivating them, because only by doing this can you possibly put things right. When it comes to health, Pluto's influence could lead to physical blockages, such as constipation. Therefore, if you're prone to this, pay attention to your diet and you should be able to sidestep any serious problems.

Neptune is breezing along in the airy sign of Aquarius this year, and that's likely to affect all the people you're financially dependent upon, such as your mate or your boss. There may be times when you will sincerely believe that they really don't know what they're doing, but it would be best not to interfere; instead, lend an ear and perhaps a helping hand whenever it is asked for. There's also a possibility that your bank, as well as all moneyed professions, may not be as efficient as usual, and so it might be a good idea to double-check all of your statements in order to help offset this difficulty.

Uranus, too, is drifting along in the air sign of Aquarius, so once more people you are financially dependent upon are highlighted. They may be suffering from stresses and strains on and off throughout this year; therefore, it would be a good idea to forget your own troubles when you notice this is happening, and be as sympathetic and as thoughtful as you possibly can. Your boss may be going through a hard time; remember that being in a more elevated position than yourself doesn't make him or her immune to bugs, germs and general stress. Should he or she display any uncharacteristic behaviour, it might be politic for you to ignore it, rather than sulking or making a big fuss.

That mighty planet, Saturn, is to be found drifting along in the earthy sign of Taurus during the first few months of the year. This is the area of your chart devoted to friends and acquaintances, and it may be that you'll be more attracted to people who are perhaps older and more experienced than yourself. There's a lot to be learnt from them, and it's up to you whether or not you are prepared to open up your mind to take on board everything that the stars are throwing at you.

Lucky Jupiter is in the airy sign of Gemini for the first half of the year, which is a rather quiet and secretive part of your chart. This seems to be hinting that the good luck is to be found behind the scenes in some way, or maybe through the use of your own very active imagination. Don't be afraid to express any ideas that you may have, because they are certainly going to be far more appreciated than usual. Jupiter so placed may also affect your health. Of course, you always like to indulge in excesses, but this planet is not giving you permission to go overboard; instead it is advising common sense and moderation, because only in this way will you get through 2001 as fit as a fiddle. When exceptions to this arise and you're suffering from tummy bugs or perhaps headaches, then you can be quite sure that it's because you are playing your own worst enemy, something that a Cancer is fairly expert at. As long as you try to control this tendency, there's no reason why you shouldn't enjoy the year 2001 and get a great deal out of it.

Career Year

YOU USUALLY FIND SUCCESS, because you have tremendous tenacity. You know what you want, and you cling on until you get it; you devote your entire self to perfection and feel uncomfortable with a lesser performance.

You are hard-working, highly organized and a person who knows how to make your shrewd good sense work best for you. You're able to assess any business situation, and because of this you are frequently far ahead of associates and competitors. However, you still suffer from insecurity that you may not be as good as you'd like to be.

You're the type of person to bring the office home with you and to agonize in the middle of the night about a minor detail left undone. When emotionally involved in perfecting your professional performance, you work overtime, even on weekends. Nothing will persuade you into lightening your load once you've made some sort of commitment to it.

Careers in the film industry frequently fascinate your sign, because of the intensity of the creativity and competition. You could also survive in a bristling business environment, but you will first have to harden your feelings and desensitize your emotions. You'd make an excellent executive, because you are highly organized and extremely hard-working. Also, work with the public in politics or economics could be quite appealing.

However, what about the year ahead?

Well, up until 20 January you'll do exceptionally well if you're in any kind of professional partnership; your ability to give and take will be appreciated by everyone around.

From 20 January through to 18 February, it is those of you involved in finances, such as bankers, who will be doing particularly well.

From 19 February through to 20 March, it's the Crab who works in importing or exporting, foreign affairs or higher education who can expect to do well. If you're taking any kind of test at this time, you'll have no problems whatsoever, providing you have boned up properly.

From 21 March through to 20 April, you'll be extremely intense, very ambitious and almost impossible to beat, regardless of the job you do. Rivals and competitors are likely to fall by the wayside at this time.

From 21 April through to 20 May, Cancerians who work either as part of a team or perhaps in administration will be doing exceptionally well.

From 21 May through to 21 June, your imagination will know no bounds. It's an exceptionally good time for research, too, and anything which requires a touch of originality will be paying off.

From 22 June through to 22 July, the Sun will, of course, be in your sign. This means it's a good time for the freelance worker, who may find offers coming in from all sides. It will be exceptionally fruitful, too, if you happen to be in a position of authority where others need you to take the lead, which you will do with aplomb.

From 23 July through to 23 August, it will be the Crab who is employed in the money profession who will be the most successful.

From 24 August to 22 September, the signs bode well for the estate agent, the property tycoon and those who improve other people's homes, such as the interior decorator, painter or plumber.

From 23 September to 23 October, it seems to be an exceptionally lucky time for the Crab who is at all artistic, sporty, or perhaps those involved with children. All of these groups should push ahead.

From 24 October through to 22 November, Cancerians who provide any kind of service are likely to be thriving. Work colleagues will be only too willing to help you out in any way they can.

From 23 November through to 21 December, there will be more cooperation between yourself and other people, so it's a good time for the freelance worker and for those in partnership.

All in all, then, your career year seems to be on the up and up, and all you need is an extra bit of confidence to push it that step further.

Money Year

WHEN EVERYTHING ELSE in your life seems unsettled, you're the type of person who tends to turn to money as a security blanket. Plenty of cash is a means to greater independence, since you hate borrowing and being in any kind of debt.

You are shrewd enough to be a financial wizard and are the kind of person most likely to get rich quick, because you don't try to.

Even if you had a million, you'd still live in fear that inflation might dog your step. Some Crabs are downright cheap, others are cautious. However, since those born under this sign are pleasure-loving people, you don't hold back from spending your money on what makes you happy, although you may haggle with the local grocer over the price of his produce.

You're far too emotional for money ever to bring you real happiness. What it will bring, though, is a good deal of satisfaction from the sense of security and the creature comforts it provides.

But what about the year ahead?

Well, your financial planet is the Sun, and this heavenly orb moves pretty quickly in comparison to some of the others, so it's not surprising that life is frequently up and down for you where cash matters are concerned.

From 1 to 20 January, the Sun occupies Capricorn, your opposite sign. Therefore, you're quite likely to gain through ideas and suggestions from other people, so make sure that you listen to them.

February finds the Sun situated in Aquarius until the 19th. There is an indication here that, although you may not be thriving yourself, the people you are financially dependent upon are at their most generous and successful, and, of course, this will rub off on you.

March finds the Sun in Pisces up until the 20th, and that's the part of your chart devoted to foreign affairs and higher education, so both themes are likely to be dominant and extremely lucky for you.

For the majority of April the Sun will be coasting along in Aries, the zenith point of your chart. Therefore, cash matters are likely to assume great importance and are bound to be successful, although, of course, there will be the odd days when bad luck could strike, and these can be found in the *Monthly* and *Daily Guides*.

During May the Sun will be drifting along in Taurus. This is the part of your chart devoted to friends and acquaintances, so keep your eyes and ears open at all times, because you could be picking up useful tips, although we're not talking about gambling here.

June finds the Sun in Gemini early in the month, and that's a rather secretive part of your chart, and one which represents what's going on in the background. Clearly, then, this is a time for keeping your ears and eyes peeled.

July is probably one of the most successful parts of the year, because the Sun is in your sign. Consequently, financial opportunities are likely to come in left, right and centre. If you decide to purchase anything, you'll be looking for good value, as indeed is always the case with you.

August is a time when you'll decide to save. Perhaps you've had an early holiday, or maybe there have been other expenses, and now you are getting a little bit insecure, which is very common with people born under your sign.

September's stars suggest that you could do quite well for yourself by a clever bit of buying, selling and negotiation.

October sees money being spent on the family, on the home and perhaps on property too. However, it doesn't look as if anything is going to waste, which is, of course, a good thing.

November is a time when you'll decide to be a little bit more generous, and you could throw caution to the wind by spending on children, partying and on your appearance too. But, of course, you'll shop around as you always do.

December is an expensive month for everyone, but this year you have vowed not to waste money as you sometimes do, and just for once you'll be able to stick to it.

Love And Sex Year

LOVE IS EXTREMELY IMPORTANT TO YOU: without it you frequently feel that the fates are going against you and become rather depressed. Your greatest fear is probably growing old with no-one to love you.

Love and romance are the nourishment that revitalizes your soul and gives you energy to interact with the world with greater zest and vitality. Often you seem to insulate your deepest emotions in a tight bond of trust and sharing.

You're a highly emotional individual who often allows sentiment to saturate your romantic experiences. Therefore, it is not unlikely that you have suffered some bitter disappointment because of your relentless subjectivity. As a defence against your vulnerability, you sometimes appear cool, aloof and uncaring. Less intuitive individuals are puzzled by your enigmatic behaviour and react defensively to it. However, you're not cold at all: you're merely being cautious, perhaps because you've been hurt too many times.

So, what are your chances of finding romance during the year ahead?

Well, the planet which rules other people in your life is Saturn, and from January until 20 April it will be in the earthy sign of Taurus. There's a suggestion here that friends and acquaintances may make some introductions to you which could be important.

From 21 April through to the end of the year, Saturn will be in Gemini, so emotional and sexual matters may not be quite so straightforward. Much seems to be going on in the background, and you must take care that others do not pull the wool over your eyes. Still, if you use the *Monthly* and *Daily Guides* I think it unlikely that you'll go too wrong; caution is, of course, your watchword where personal matters are concerned.

The position of Venus has a great deal of influence on our personal lives. During January it will be coasting along in Pisces, and as a result you could be strongly attracted to people who come from very different backgrounds, such as foreigners.

During February Venus can be found in the fiery sign of Aries. That's the zenith point of your chart, so work matters and emotional affairs seem to be intertwined here.

Venus continues in Aries through March, but unfortunately it goes into retrograde action, so it would not be a good idea to become romantically involved with colleagues at this time. Venus remains in Aries through April and May, so the trend towards mixing business with pleasure continues through to 7th June, when Venus will be moving into Taurus. After this, friends and acquaintances will be making introductions, so be as sociable as you possibly can.

July brings a warning that is that nothing will be straightforward where emotions are concerned: either you or other people could be deceptive, and you need to be on your guard.

Early August sees Venus moving into your sign, so you're looking good and feeling good. This is a wonderful time for forming all kinds of relationships, be they professional or personal.

September is a very casual month for matters of the heart. You'll be taking your romance and perhaps your sex on the run, as it were, but you won't be taking anything too seriously.

October seems to be a quiet month; your priorities are lying elsewhere, although no doubt the *Daily Guides* will throw up the odd day which you can utilize.

From 9 November through to 2 December you're in a happy-go-lucky mood, attending parties, reluctant to make commitments and preferring to play with multiple admirers, rather than concentrating on anyone in particular.

From 3 December through to the end of the year, romance and love can be found in connection with your colleagues and also whilst going about your professional duties. Naturally, there will be particular dates that you should watch out for, and these can be found in the *Monthly* and *Daily Guides*.

Health And Diet Year

YOUR SIGN RULES A WIDE AND VARIED array of functions. It has dominion over the brain, lung and heart membranes, sinus cavities, eyeballs, bone marrow, the cheeks, and glycogen stored in the liver.

Your sign's primary area is the stomach and the digestive organs. Typical health problems of this sign include digestive ailments, gastric mucus, and cravings for alcohol. The peristalsis, or digestive contractions, of the stomach are ruled by your sign. Without good thorough peristalsis, the food is not broken down properly before entering the stomach and intestinal tracts, where nutrition is absorbed so that it can be used by the body. However, fortunately, your body responds to common sense: therefore, if you eat sensibly and drink moderately, in the main you can stay perfectly healthy.

But what about the year ahead?

Well, during January, Mars will be situated in Scorpio. The biggest problem here could be overindulgence when out partying, and also, perhaps, minor sporting accidents.

The biggest danger to health in February is simply exhaustion. You are certainly in control here, so do be sensible.

During March there are certain complications in your

love life, as well as too much physical activity, especially where sports are concerned, and both of these could undermine your health.

April brings a great deal of socializing where work matters are concerned, but don't overdo it. Not only will your body suffer, but you could also make a fool of yourself if you drink too much.

May seems to be a relatively healthy time, although you may be suffering from mental frustration because things aren't running as smoothly as you would like.

Mercury is in retrograde action for part of June, so once again frustration could set your nerves jangling.

Fortunately, there's not a great deal wrong with July: you look and feel good and are ready to take on the world single-handed.

August, too, looks to be promising, the only danger being the possibility that you could overindulge in food and alcohol.

In September, Mars will be in your opposite sign, so you must be especially careful in situations where minor accidents could occur, such as when handling hot or sharp objects.

October could bring a certain amount of frustration with other people, and this could wear you out from time to time, but it's nothing serious.

A retrograde Saturn in November may lead to more frustration in connection with other people, but this is unlikely to undermine your health for more than a day or so.

In December, there's precious little for you to worry about, apart from a tendency to be having too much fun: but then, why shouldn't you? All in all, you should end this year in fine condition.

Numerology Year

IN ORDER TO DISCOVER the number of any year you are interested in, your 'individual year number', first take your birth date, day and month, and add this to the year you are interested in, be it in the past or in the future. As an example, say you were born on 13 September and you are interested in the year 2001:

$$
\begin{array}{r}
13 \\
9 \\
2001 \\
\hline
2023 \\
\hline
\end{array}
$$

Then, write down $2 + 0 + 2 + 3$ and you will discover this equals 7. This means that the number of your year is 7. If the number adds up to more than 9, add these two digits together.

You can experiment with this method by taking any year from your past and following this guide to find whether or not numerology works out for you.

The guide is perennial and applicable to all Sun signs: you can look up years for your friends as well as for yourself.

Use it to discover general trends ahead, the way you should be approaching a chosen period and how you can make the most of the future.

Individual Year Number 1

General Feel

A time for being more self-sufficient and one when you should be ready to grasp the nettle. All opportunities must be snapped up, after careful consideration. Also an excellent time for laying down the foundations for future success in all areas.

Definition

Because this is the number 1 individual year, you will have the chance to start again in many areas of life. The emphasis will be upon the new; there will be fresh faces in your life, more opportunities and perhaps even new experiences. If you were born on either the 1st, 19th or 28th and were born under the sign of Aries or Leo then this will be an extremely important time. It is crucial during this cycle that you be prepared to go it alone, push back horizons and generally open up your mind. Time also for playing the leader or pioneer wherever necessary. If you have a hobby which you wish to turn into a business, or maybe you simply wish to introduce other people to your ideas and plans, then do so whilst experiencing this individual cycle. A great period too for laying down the plans for long-term future gains. Therefore, make sure you do your homework well and you will reap the rewards at a later date.

Relationships

This is an ideal period for forming new bonds, perhaps business relationships, new friends and new loves too. You will be attracted to those in high positions and with strong personalities. There may also be an emphasis on bonding with people a good deal younger than yourself. If you are already in a long-standing relationship, then it is time to clear away the dead wood between you which may have been causing misunderstandings and unhappiness. Whether in love or business, you will find those who are born under the sign of Aries, Leo or Aquarius far more common in your life, also those born on the following dates: 1st, 4th, 9th, 10th, 13th, 18th, 19th, 22nd and 28th. The most important months for this individual year, when you are likely to meet up with those who have a strong influence on you, are January, May, July and October.

Career

It is likely that you have been wanting to break free and to explore fresh horizons in your job or in your career, and this is definitely a year for doing so. Because you are in a fighting mood, and because your decision-making qualities as well as your leadership qualities are foremost, it will be an easy matter for you to find assistance as well as to impress other people. Major professional changes are likely and you will also feel more independent within your existing job. Should you want times for making important career moves, then choose Mondays or Tuesdays. These are good days for pushing your luck and presenting your ideas well. Changes connected with your career are going to be more likely during April, May, July and September.

Health

If you have forgotten the name of your doctor or dentist, then this is the year for going for checkups. A time too when people of a certain age are likely to start wearing glasses. The emphasis seems to be on the eyes. Start a good health regime. This will help you cope with any adverse events that almost assuredly lie ahead. The important months for your own health as well as for that of loved ones are March, May and August.

Individual Year Number 2

General Feel

You will find it far easier to relate to other people.

Definition

What you will need during this cycle is diplomacy, cooperation and the ability to put yourself in someone else's shoes. Whatever you began last year will now begin to show signs of progress. However, don't expect miracles; changes are going to be slow rather than at the speed of light. Changes will be taking place all around you. It is possible too that you will be considering moving from one area to another, maybe even to another country. There is a lively feel about domesticity and in relationships with the opposite sex too. This is going to be a marvellous year for making dreams come true and asking for favours. However, on no account should you force yourself and your opinions on other people. A spoonful of honey is going to get you a good deal further than a spoonful of vinegar. If you are born under the sign of Cancer or Taurus, or if your birthday falls on the

2nd, 11th, 20th or 29th, then this year is going to be full of major events.

Relationships

You need to associate with other people far more than usual – perhaps out of necessity. The emphasis is on love, friendship and professional partnerships. The opposite sex will be much more prepared to get involved in your life than is normally the case. This is a year your chances of becoming engaged or married are increased and there is likely to be an increase in your family in the form of a lovely addition and also in the families of your friends and those closest to you. The instinctive and caring side to your personality is going to be strong and very obvious. You will quickly discover that you will be particularly touchy and sensitive to things that other people say. Further, you will find those born under the sign of Cancer, Taurus and Libra entering your life far more than usual. This also applies to those who are born on the 2nd, 6th, 7th, 11th, 15th, 20th, 24th, 25th or 29th of the month.

Romantic and family events are likely to be emphasized during April, June and September.

Career

There is a strong theme of change here, but there is no point in having a panic attack about that because, after all, life is about change. However, in this particular year any transformation or upheaval is likely to be of an internal nature, such as at your place of work, rather than external. You may find your company is moving from one area to another, or perhaps there are changes between departments. Quite obviously, then, the most important thing for you to do in order to make your life easy is to be adaptable. There is a strong possibility too that you may be given added responsibility. Do not flinch as this will bring in extra reward.

If you are thinking of searching for employment this year, then try to arrange all meetings and negotiations on Monday and Friday. These are good days for asking for favours or rises too. The best months are March, April, June, August, and December. All these are important times for change.

Health

This individual cycle emphasizes stomach problems. The important thing for you is to eat sensibly, rather than go on a crash diet, which could be detrimental. If you are female then you would be wise to have a checkup at least once during the year ahead just to be sure you can continue to enjoy good health. All should be discriminating when dining out. Check cutlery, and take care if food has only been partially cooked. Furthermore, emotional stress could get you down, but only if you allow it to. Provided you set aside some periods of relaxation in each day when you can close your eyes and let everything drift away, then you will have little to worry about. When it comes to diet, be sure that the emphasis is on nutrition, rather than fighting the flab. Perhaps it would be a good idea to become less weight-conscious during this period and let your body find its natural ideal weight on its own. The months of February, April, July and November may show health changes in some way. Common sense is your best guide during this year.

Individual Year Number 3

General Feel

You are going to be at your most creative and imaginative during this time. There is a theme of expansion and growth, and you will want to polish up your self-image in order to make the 'big impression'.

Definition

It is a good year for reaching out, for expansion. Social and artistic developments should be interesting as well as profitable, and this will help to promote happiness. There will be a strong urge in you to improve yourself, either your image, your reputation or perhaps your mind. Your popularity soars through the ceiling and this delights you. Involving yourself with something creative brings increased success plus a good deal of satisfaction. However, it is imperative that you keep yourself in a positive mood. This will attract attention and appreciation of all of your talents. Projects which were begun two years ago are likely to be bearing fruit this year. If you are born under the sign of Pisces or Sagittarius, or your birthday falls on the 3rd, 12th, 21st or 30th, then this year is going to be particularly special and successful.

Relationships

There is a happy-go-lucky feel about all your relationships and you are in a flirty, fancy-free mood. Heaven help anyone trying to catch you during the next twelve months: they will need to get their skates on. Relationships are likely to be light-hearted and fun rather than heavy going. It is possible too that you will find yourself with those who are younger than you, particularly those born under the signs of Pisces and Sagittarius, and those whose birth dates add up to 3, 6 or 9. Your individual cycle shows important months for relationships are March, May, August and December.

Career

As I discussed earlier, this individual number is one that suggests branching out and personal growth, so be ready to take on anything new. Not surprisingly, your career aspects look bright and shiny. You are definitely going to be more ambitious and must keep up that positive facade and attract opportunities. Avoid taking obligations too lightly; it is important that you adopt a conscientious approach to all your responsibilities. You may take on a fresh course of learning or look for a new job, and the important days for doing so would be on Thursday and Friday: these are definitely your best days. This is particularly true in the months of February, March, May, July and November: expect expansion in your life and take a chance during these times.

Health

Because you are likely to be out and about painting the town all the colours of the rainbow, it is likely that health problems could come through overindulgence or perhaps tiredness. However, if you have got to have some health problems, I suppose these are the best ones to experience, because they are under your control. There is also a possibility that you may get a little fraught over work, which may result in some emotional scenes. However, you are sensible enough to realize they should not be taken too seriously. If you are prone to skin allergies, then these too could be giving you problems during this particular year. The best advice you can follow is not to go to extremes that will affect your body or your mind. It is all very well to have fun, but after a while too much of it not only affects your health but also the degree of enjoyment you experience. Take extra care between January and March, and June and October, especially where these are winter months for you.

Individual Year Number 4

General Feel
It is back to basics this year. Do not build on shaky foundations. Get yourself organized and be prepared to work a little harder than you usually do and you will come through without any great difficulty.

Definition
It is imperative that you have a grand plan. Do not simply rush off without considering the consequences and avoid dabbling of any kind. It is likely too that you will be gathering more responsibility, and on occasions this could lead you to feeling unappreciated, claustrophobic and perhaps overburdened in some ways. Although it is true to say that this cycle in your individual life tends to bring about a certain amount of limitation, whether this be on the personal, the psychological or the financial side to life, you now have the chance to get yourself together and to build on more solid foundations. Security is definitely your key word at this time. When it comes to any project, or job or plan, it is important that you ask the right questions. In other words do your homework before you go off half-cocked. That would be a disaster. If you

are an Aquarius, a Leo or a Gemini or you are born on the 4th, 13th, 22nd, or 31st of any month, this individual year will be extremely important and long remembered.

Relationships

You will find that it is the eccentric, the unusual, the unconventional and the downright odd that will be drawn into your life during this particular cycle. It is also strongly possible that people you have not met for some time may be re-entering your circle and an older person or somebody outside your own social or perhaps religious background will be drawn to you too. When it comes to the romantic side of life, again you are drawn to that which is different from usual. You may even form a relationship with someone who comes from a totally different background, perhaps from far away. Something unusual about them stimulates and excites you. Gemini, Leo and Aquarius are your likely favourites, as well as anyone whose birth number adds up to 1, 4, 5 or 7. Certainly the most exciting months for romance are going to be February, April, July and November. Make sure then that you socialize a lot during this particular time, and be ready for literally anything.

Career

Once more we have the theme of the unusual and different in this area of life. You may be plodding along in the same old rut when suddenly lightning strikes and you find yourself besieged by offers from other people and, in a panic, not quite sure what to do. There may be a period when nothing particular seems to be going on when to your astonishment you are given a promotion or some exciting challenge. Literally anything can happen in this particular cycle of your life. The individual year 4 also inclines towards added responsibilities, and it is important that you do not off-load them onto other people or cringe in fear. They will eventually pay off and in the meantime you will be gaining in experience and paving the way for greater success in the future. When you want to arrange any kind of meeting, negotiation or perhaps ask for a favour at work, then try to do so on a Monday or a Wednesday for the luckiest results. January, February, April, October and November are certainly the months when you must play the opportunist and be ready to say yes to anything that comes your way.

Health

The biggest problems that you will have to face this year are caused by stress, so it is important that you attend to your diet and take life as philosophically as possible, as well as being ready to adapt to changing conditions. You are likely to find that people you thought you knew well are acting out of character and this throws you off balance. Take care, too, when visiting the doctor. Remember that you are dealing with a human being and that doctors, like the rest of us, can make mistakes. Unless you are 100 per cent satisfied then go for a second opinion over anything important. Try to be sceptical about yourself because you are going to be a good deal more moody than usual. The times that need special attention are February, May, September and November. If any of these months fall in the winter part of your year, then wrap up well and dose up on vitamin C.

Individual Year Number 5

General Feel

There will be many more opportunities for you to get out and about and travel is certainly going to be playing a large part in your year. Change too must be expected and even embraced – after all, it is part of life. You will have more free time and choices, so all in all things look promising.

Definition

It is possible that you tried previously to get something off the launching pad, but for one reason or another it simply didn't happen. Luckily, you now get a chance to renew those old plans and put them into action. You are certainly going to feel that things are changing for the better in all areas. You are going to be more actively involved with the public and will enjoy a certain amount of attention and publicity. You may have failed in the past, but this year mistakes will be easier to accept and learn from; you are going to find yourself both physically and mentally more in tune with your environment and with those you care about than ever before. If you are a Gemini or a Virgo or are born on the 5th, 14th or 23rd then this is going to be a period of major importance for you and you must be ready to take advantage of this.

Relationships

Lucky you! Your sexual magnetism goes through the ceiling and you will be involved in many relationships during the year ahead. You have that extra charisma about you which will be attracting others, and you can look forward to being choosy. There will be an inclination to be drawn to those who are considerably younger than yourself. It is likely too that you will find that those born under the signs of Taurus, Gemini, Virgo and Libra as well as those whose birth date adds up to 2, 5 or 6 will play an important part in your year. The months for attracting others in a big way are January, March, June, October and December.

Career

This is considered by all numerologists as being one of the best numbers for self-improvement in all areas, but particularly on the professional front. It will be relatively easy for you to sell your ideas and yourself, as well as to push your skills and expertise under the noses of other people. They will certainly sit up and take notice. Clearly, then, a time for you to view the world as your oyster and to get out there and grab your piece of the action. You have increased confidence and should be able to get exactly what you want. Friday and Wednesday are perhaps the best days if looking for a job or going to negotiations or interviews, or in fact for generally pushing yourself into the limelight. Watch out for March, May, September, October or December. Something of great importance could pop up at this time. There will certainly be a chance for advancement; whether you take it or not is, of course, entirely up to you.

Health

Getting a good night's rest could be your problem during the year ahead, since that mind of yours is positively buzzing and won't let you rest. Try turning your brain off at bedtime, otherwise you will finish up irritable and exhausted. Try to take things a step at a time without rushing around. Meditation may help you to relax and do more for your physical wellbeing than anything else. Because this is an extremely active year, you will need to do some careful planning so that you can cope with ease rather than rushing around like a demented mayfly. Furthermore, try to avoid going over the top with alcohol, food, sex, gambling or anything which could be described as 'get rich quick'. During January, April, August, and October, watch yourself a bit: you could do with some coddling, particularly if these happen to be winter months for you.

Individual Year Number 6

General Feel
There is likely to be increased responsibility and activity within your domestic life. There will be many occasions when you will be helping loved ones and your sense of duty is going to be strong.

Definition
Activities for the most part are likely to be centred around property, family, loved ones, romance and your home. Your artistic appreciation will be good and you will be drawn to anything that is colourful and beautiful, and possessions that have a strong appeal to your eye or even your ear. Where domesticity is concerned, there is a strong suggestion that you may move out of one home into another. This is an excellent time too for self-education, for branching out, for graduating, for taking on some extra courses – whether simply to improve your appearance or to improve your mind. When it comes to your social life, you are inundated with chances to attend events. You are going to be a real social butterfly, flitting from scene to scene and enjoying yourself

thoroughly. Try to accept nine out of ten invitations that come your way because they bring with them chances of advancement. If you are born on the 6th, 15th or 24th or should your birth sign be Taurus, Libra or Cancer then this is going to be a year that will be long remembered as a very positive one.

Relationships

When it comes to love, sex and romance, the individual year 6 is perhaps the most successful. It is a time for being swept off your feet, for becoming engaged or even getting married. On the more negative side, perhaps there is a separation and divorce. However, the latter can be avoided, provided you are prepared to sit down and communicate properly. There is an emphasis too on pregnancy and birth, or changes in existing relationships. Circumstances will be sweeping you along. If you are born under the sign of Taurus, Cancer or Libra, then it is even more likely that this will be a major year for you, as well as for those born on dates adding up to 6, 3 or 2. The most memorable months of your year are going to be February, May, September and November. Grab all opportunities to enjoy yourself and improve your relationships during these periods.

Career

A good year for this side to life too, with the chances of promotion and recognition for past efforts all coming your way. You will be able to improve your position in life even though it is likely that recently you have been disappointed. On the cash front, big rewards will come flooding in, mainly because you are prepared to fulfil your obligations and commitments without complaint or protest. Other people will appreciate all the efforts you have put in, so plod along and you will find your efforts will not have been in vain. If you are looking for a job or setting up an interview, negotiation or a meeting, or simply want to advertise your talents in some way, then your best days for doing so are Monday, Thursday and Friday. Long-term opportunities are very strong during the months of February, April, August, September and November. These are the key periods for pushing yourself up the ladder of success.

Health

If you are to experience any problems of a physical nature during this year, then they could be tied up with the throat, nose or the tonsils, plus the upper parts of the body. Basically, what you need to stay healthy during this year is plenty of sunlight, moderate exercise, fresh air and changes of scene. Escape to the coast if this is at all possible. The months for being particularly watchful are March, July, September and December. Think twice before doing anything during these times, and there is no reason why you shouldn't stay hale and hearty for the whole year.

Individual Year Number 7

General Feel

A year for inner growth and for finding out what really makes you tick and what you need to make you happy. Self-awareness and discovery are all emphasized during the individual year 7.

Definition

You will be provided with the opportunity to place as much emphasis as possible on your personal life and your own wellbeing. There will be many occasions when you will find yourself analysing your past motives and actions, and giving more attention to your own personal needs, goals and desires. There will also be many occasions when you will want to escape any kind of confusion, muddle or noise; time spent alone will not be wasted. This will give you the chance to meditate and also to examine exactly where you have come to so far, and where you want to go in the future. It is important you make up your mind what you want out of this particular year, because once you have done so you will attain those ambitions. Failure to do this could mean you end up chasing your own tail, and that is a pure waste of time and energy. You will also discover that secrets about yourself and other people could be surfacing during this year. If you are born under the sign of Pisces or Cancer, or on the 7th, 16th or 25th of the month, then this year will be especially wonderful.

Relationships

It has to be said from the word go that this is not the best year for romantic interest. A strong need for contemplation will mean spending time on your own. Any romance that does develop this year may not live up to your expectations, but, providing you are prepared to take things as they come without jumping to conclusions, then you will enjoy yourself without getting hurt. Decide exactly what it is you have in mind and then go for it. Romantic interests this year are likely to be with people who are born on dates that add up to 2, 4 or 7 or with people born under the sign of Cancer or

Pisces. Watch for romantic opportunities during January, April, August and October.

Career

When we pass through this particular individual cycle, two things tend to occur: retirement from the limelight, and a general slowing down, perhaps by taking leave of absence or maybe retraining in some way. It is likely too that you will become more aware of your own occupational expertise and skills: you will begin to understand your true purpose in life and will feel much more enlightened. Long-sought-after goals begin to come to life if you have been drifting of late. The best attitude to have throughout this year is an exploratory one when it comes to your work. If you want to set up negotiations, interviews or meetings, arrange them for Monday or Friday. In fact, any favours you seek should be tackled on these days. January, March, July, August, October and December are particularly good for self-advancement.

Health

Since, in comparison to previous years, this is a rather quiet time, health problems are likely to be minor. Some will possibly come through irritation or worry, and the best thing to do is to attempt to remain meditative and calm. This state of mind will bring positive results. Failure to do so may create unnecessary problems by allowing your imagination to run completely out of control. You need time this year to restore, recuperate and contemplate. Any health changes that do occur are likely to happen in February, June, August and November.

Individual Year Number 8

General Feel

This is going to be a time for success, for making important moves and changes, a time when you may gain power, and certainly one when your talents are going to be recognized.

Definition

This individual year gives you the chance to 'think big'; it is a time when you can occupy the limelight and wield power. If you were born on the 8th, 17th or 26th of the month or come under the sign of Capricorn, pay attention to this year and make sure you make the most of it. You should develop greater maturity and discover a true feeling of faith and destiny, both in yourself and in events that occur. This part of the cycle is connected with career, ambition and money, but debts from the past will have to be repaid. For example, an old responsibility or debt that you may have avoided in past years could reappear to haunt you. However, whatever you do with these twelve months, aim high: think big, think success and above all be positive.

Relationships

This particular year is one which is strongly connected with birth, divorce and marriage: most of the landmarks we experience in life, in fact. When it comes to love, those who are more experienced or older than you, or people of power, authority, influence or wealth will be very attractive. This year will be putting you back in touch with those from your past – old friends, comrades, associates, and even romances from long ago crop up once more. You should not experience any great problems romantically this year, especially if you are dealing with Capricorns or Librans, or with those whose date of birth adds up to 8, 6 or 3. The best months for romance to develop are likely to be March, July, September and December.

Career

The number 8 year is generally believed to be the best one when it comes to bringing in cash. It is also good for asking for a rise or achieving promotion or authority over other people. This is your year for basking in the limelight of success, the result perhaps of your past efforts. Now you will be rewarded. Financial success is all but guaranteed, provided you keep faith with your ambitions and yourself. It is important that you set major goals for yourself and work slowly towards them. You will be surprised how easily they are fulfilled. Conversely, if you are looking for work, then do set up interviews, negotiations and meetings, preferably on Saturday, Thursday or Friday, which are your luckiest days. Also watch out for chances to do yourself a bit of good during February, June, July, September and November.

Health

You can avoid most health problems, particularly headaches, constipation or liver problems, by avoiding depression and feelings of loneliness. It is important when these descend that you keep yourself busy enough not to dwell on them. When it comes to receiving attention from the medical profession, you would be well advised to get a second opinion. Eat wisely, try to keep a positive and enthusiastic outlook on life and all will be well. Periods which need special care are January, May, July and October. Therefore, if these months fall during the winter part of your year, wrap up well and dose yourself with vitamins.

Individual Year Number 9

General Feel

A time for tying up loose ends. Wishes are likely to be fulfilled and matters brought to swift conclusions. Inspiration runs amok. Much travel is likely.

Definition

The number 9 individual year is perhaps the most successful of all. It tends to represent the completion of matters, whether in work, business, or personal affairs. Your ability to let go of habits, people and negative circumstances or situations that may have been holding you back is strong. The sympathetic and humane side to your character also surfaces, and you learn to give more freely of yourself without expecting anything in return. Any good deeds that you do will certainly be well rewarded, in terms of satisfaction and perhaps financially too. If you are born under the sign of Aries or Scorpio, or on the 9th, 18th or 27th of the month, this is certainly going to be an all-important year.

Relationships

The individual year 9 is a cycle which gives appeal as well as influence. Because of this, you will be getting emotionally tied up with members of the opposite sex who may be outside your usual cultural or ethnic group. The reason for this is that this particular number relates to humanity, and of course this tends to quash ignorance, pride and bigotry. You also discover that Aries, Leo and Scorpio people are going to be much more evident in your domestic affairs, as well as those whose birth dates add up to 9, 3 or 1. The important months for relationships are February, June, August and

November. These will be extremely hectic and eventful from a romantic viewpoint and there are times when you could be swept off your feet.

Career

This is a year which will help to make many of your dreams and ambitions come true. Furthermore, it is an excellent time for success if you are involved in marketing your skills, talents and expertise more widely. You may be thinking of expanding abroad for example and, if so, this is certainly a good idea. You will find that harmony and cooperation with your fellow workers are easier than before and this will help your dreams and ambitions. The best days for you if you want to line up meetings or negotiations are going to be Tuesday and Thursday, and this also applies if you are looking for employment or want a special day for doing something of an ambitious nature. Employment or business changes could also feature during January, May, June, August and October.

Health

The only physical problems you may have during this particular year will be because of accidents, so be careful. Try too to avoid unnecessary tension and arguments with other people. Take extra care when you are on the roads: no drinking and driving, for example. You will only have problems if you play your own worst enemy. Be extra careful when in the kitchen or bathroom: sharp instruments that you find in these areas could lead to cuts unless you take care.

Your Sun Sign Partner

Cancer with Cancer

You are a cosy couple who probably never leave the house unless you absolutely have to. Both of you are domestic types who would just as soon cook in than be taken out to the most elegant of restaurants. You share the same dewy-eyed sentimentalism, shower each other with tender expressions of love, and emotionally empathize in those moody moments that seem like they're never going to subside.

This is a relationship of deep understanding, a high degree of compatibility and a plethora of physical passion. Because of the intense rapport and the feelings of selfless caring, it could last a lifetime.

Cancer Woman

Cancer woman with Aries man

She'll fall in love with his dynamic enthusiasm, but may get hurt by his lack of emotional understanding. She needs more nurturing than he knows how to give and has more insecurities than he knows how to handle. He'll blunder his way through her life, and she'll hold back the tears when she sees him leaving (even for five minutes). He can't understand why she's so emotional, and sometimes he feels closed off and closed in.

She's one woman who will stick by him for better or worse. She will support him with a sincerity that he might find irresistible and will love him with a loyalty that inspires his respect. However, whether he will stick by her is quite another matter.

Cancer woman with Taurus man

You are two stay-at-home creatures and can have a lovely evening just preparing a pot of stew. At times she will remind him of his mother at Christmas. He will remind her of Daddy on the days that he paid the rent. In each other they find their fantasies of security are satisfied, and for both that means a lot. She'll find him to be someone solid to lean on, while he will find her a cushion of kindness.

She will want to be possessed by him for ever. He wants someone to treat him like his savings account. Deep down inside, he dreams of a 'little woman', and even if she were president of a multinational corporation, she would still be willing to take on the traditional role. These two were made for each other and could spend a lifetime loving. All that they have to do is meet.

Cancer woman with Gemini man

She's a homely person, but he can't be in enough places at once. She is shy, deeply emotional and very moody; he is detached, cerebral and very changeable. These two are a gnawing enigma to each other in the best moments and a murderous annoyance in the worst. She craves emotional security, but he lives for his freedom. She needs to be made to feel secure, while he needs to be challenged.

Emotionally, this is about the least compatible combination in the zodiac. However, for this very reason they could be very good for each other if they are both willing to try. He could realize that he really has got feelings underneath his overworked mind, and she might realize that she really has got a sense of humour underneath all of those obsessive fears and insecurities.

Cancer woman with Leo man

It might seem to him that she wants his soul on a silver platter. She does. When it comes to love, she is a conspicuous consumer. She craves all his attention, affection, fantasies, thoughts and dreams. When she doesn't get her way, she gets weepy. At first, this is effective, but after a few similar performances, this man begins to cool off.

Her dependence will flatter him, but her demands will make him feel claustrophobic. On the first coffee date, she'll ask where he stands on their future. If he manages to get a second date, she'll ask him if he prefers a wedding in June or December.

Sometimes she'll be his mother, at other times his little girl. It's very hard for her just to be a lover, because she never feels that much at ease with her own emotions. His challenge is treating her like a woman and letting her believe it. But that takes a very selfless kind of loving, and it's not clear whether Mr Leo can do it.

Cancer woman with Virgo man

Although her moods often confuse him, her intense emotions provide an encouragement that gives him tremendous comfort. He is as insecure as she is, though he covers it up with his will and his acute sense of logic. She will evoke his most vulnerable emotions, and he will help her to filter life through her head as well as her heart. However, at times, he won't be as cuddly as her affectionate nature would like. He spends most of his time working, and when he's not working, he's worrying about whether he could have done a better job.

He is an exceedingly cerebral person, whereas she is exceedingly emotional. But both of them can respect the other's perspective and can learn to work through them rather than around them. This could be a relationship of lasting value that results in a sound marriage.

Cancer woman with Libra man

She will give him all those little, mothering attentions, and she'll throw in a few more for good measure. However, after she has poured out to him endlessly, and all he has to say to her is that he can't decide what he wants in a woman, it should be a hasty goodbye. Unfortunately, she'll hang around for a few more of these tender emotional scenes.

Mr Libra considers himself to be a person with feelings. He is, but they're all about himself. It takes a lot for her to realize that it really is over, and it takes even more for Mr Libra to realize that it's even begun. The emotional timing here is so bad that it would probably take more than a lifetime for them to get together. It might be better for them to wait until their next lives, when with any luck they will be reincarnated into different signs.

Cancer woman with Scorpio man

She'll nurture his needs, make him fat and happy on her

cooking, and try to be understanding when he's being surly. She is kind, giving, compassionate, and more caring than a Red Cross nurse. She'll listen to his problems, pay him more attention than he desires or deserves, and make him feel like he's the greatest show on earth. All she wants in return is love. But she wants to be smothered in it.

He appreciates her love and affection, but something deep within him makes it difficult for him to totally accept it. He needs to keep his own space, not necessarily because he wants it, but because he has a fear that if any woman gets too close and he starts to need her, she just might be taken away.

This could be a great match, just as long as he is ready to settle for some connubial bliss. If Mr Scorpio only has a good fling in mind, then she should just keep on walking.

Cancer woman with Sagittarius man

He'll see her as a drag on his independence, and she'll see him as a threat to her tenuous sense of security. She'll be hurt and hostile when he doesn't even finish his dessert because he has a tennis game to play. His patience will be provoked when she would rather sit by the fireside than go skiing.

She seeks a quiet kind of romance with someone who will provide an array of creature comforts. He seeks a short-lived affair that is more like an animal chase. His charm will probably rip right into her soul like a grenade going off in a sleepy village. Any way you look at it, these two are about as compatible as pickles and ice cream.

Cancer woman with Capricorn man

He is the security she has always longed for, while she is the woman who can give him the warmth he so needs.

Between them there is an undeniable attraction and a very basic understanding.

Together they can live a cosy existence, showering lots of love on each other and sharing many intense moments. Within the depths of her feelings he will be able to see the same insecurities that bring on his own melancholic moments. The more they allow their sensitivities to expand into the depths of each other, the more emotionally rich their life will ultimately be. And, once they've had it, they won't be able to deny that this is the greatest kind of wealth.

Cancer woman with Aquarius man

She lives by her emotions, whereas he relies on his logic. This creates a kind of friction that may be more than either of them can stand. She may think she has to knock him out with a swift karate chop and then hypnotize him with the right words just to get a little romance going.

When she makes him a pie, he'll take it apart, stare at it for a while, ask what's in it, and then forget to eat it because he's too busy talking. Needless to say, Mr Aquarius gets more pleasure in finding out how the whole thing works than he does in the actual experience.

Although he is a good, hearty sort, he sometimes gets so entangled in his theories that he reminds her of a mad scientist who sleeps with test tubes under his pillow. If she wants a man to hug her, make mad, passionate love to her, and remind her how much she means to him, she'd better start looking in a different direction.

Cancer woman with Pisces man

He will find her nice to cuddle. She will create a plethora of seductive creature comforts and provide the emotional backup he needs to do his best. Not only is she warm and sensitive, she also has the kind of womanly strength that reminds him of his mother. She will understand his moods, listen to his problems and lend him a lot of loving assistance for those projects he knows he'll never finish.

In essence, this combination leads to a divine exploration into the deepest experience of love. Communication with him could carry her out to the farthest planes of feeling.

Cancer Man

Cancer man with Aries woman

He is a truly lovable person, but his love is not meant for her. Her fiery outbursts will send him into sullen withdrawal, and his sullen withdrawals will send her into more fiery outbursts. The two of them are so different that they seem to be coming from two foreign countries that never even knew the other existed.

Emotionally, she is supersensitive, though she hates to show it. She has a way of hurting his feelings even by the way she asks him a polite question. His feeble attempts to camouflage his vulnerability make her chew her nails. His moods make her more than impatient, and his apparent placidity makes her stamp her feet just to break the silence. If Miss Aries wants a lot of drama, she'd better go to a movie or find someone else.

Cancer man with Taurus woman

A great deal of passion will pass between these two, but whether the relationship endures depends on where they are both willing to take it.

He is loyal and loving, but the meaning of his moods will totally elude her. One moment he is insecure and dependent, and the next he is totally withdrawn. Her feelings have a way of tying them both up in knots. However, together they will satiate each other's needs for security. She is practical, while he is passionate. She is the earthy foundation to his ivory tower.

She tends to dwell on fundamentals, while he lingers on the romantic overtones. He is carried away by softness and subtlety; she is more entranced by some support. Both are so jealous that they make each other feel sought after when they trade suspicions. And both are so domestic that together they can spend a weekend cooking up a storm.

In most respects, this relationship is highly compatible, because when you combine earth with water, the result is fertility and sustained emotion.

Cancer man with Gemini woman

He is emotional and vulnerable, while outwardly she is cool and controlled. He is often victimized by his feelings, whereas she is put out of control by her mind.

This is a relationship where communication will definitely break down. He is so supersensitive that he considers her friendliness to other people purposefully insulting. And when he sulks over his steak and refuses to tell her the time, she comes to the conclusion that he would be better off with the waitress.

They have a way of bringing out each other's most painful insecurities; it's a kind of quiet emotional immolation. She has a way of laughing at times when he wants her to be serious, and he has a way of being glacial when she needs some warmth. Their only real hope is to stop chatting and start talking. Decide to be brave, put away emotional masks and supports, and try leaning on each other.

Cancer man with Leo woman

Although he loves romantic games, he is soon worn down by the reality of her emotions. He will call her twelve times a day, but she's always busy. On the first call he is extremely interested, by the sixth he is morosely impassioned, and by the ninth he has abandoned all control.

His histrionics are indecently excessive, even for her sensibilities; at his most dramatic he is dark and brooding. When his senses are unsatisfied, he melts into melancholia and defiance. He tries to get her attention by not speaking or calling. With relief, she surmises that he's finally found some self-respect. At last, when he finds that he can no longer stand it, his fingers find their way to the telephone. Assuming a cold, aloof manner, he invites her to the south of France for the weekend. She tells him that she has to wash her hair. What he doesn't realize is that, even if her love life is nonexistent, she won't persuade herself to consider him.

Cancer man with Virgo woman

He'll make her feel like a nineteenth-century femme fatale in a picture hat. He'll heartily respond to her shyness, her little insecurities, her warmth, and the way she blushes when he compliments her. She'll love the way he courts her. She'll treasure his concern when she has a slight cold, and she'll be thankful for the way his affection makes her feel appreciated at last.

For one of the few times in her life, she feels secure in her feelings, while he feels that this is a fantasy he's always hoped for. Together, they can take each other to many wondrous emotional places and enjoy a kind of happiness they have never had before.

Cancer man with Libra woman

He'll give her all the attention she craves and will delight in creating those cosy stay-at-home evenings she loves. At dinner parties, he'll help her cook and will probably make a few gastronomic delights of his own. However, he will question why she has to spend several hundred pounds on saucepans and an only slightly smaller amount on new boots when last year's still look perfectly good. There will be moments when his moodiness will make her morose. But none of this will diminish the joy they can experience together.

He's sensitive, kind and caring, and she can help him restore his emotional balance. He wants a woman he can be secure with; she wants the same from a man, as well as the pleasures of shared experience. Together, they could create a romance of which dreams are made. And with all his charm, it's an easy task to transform a dream into a romantic reality.

Cancer man with Scorpio woman

For her, he's a package deal: a man with the qualities of a mother. He'll understand her moods, kiss her on the temples, bake her apple pie and serve her tea with lemon. This combination is highly compatible, especially if she was born in the last ten days of the Scorpio period.

As long as she respects his feelings, he'll be kind and caring, and happy to be controlled by her feminine power. Once she makes him feel secure, he will be loyal, proud and possessive. He'll romance her personality and give her total power. He'll let her take him wherever she wants to go and make it known that she is the journey that he has always wanted to take.

Cancer man with Sagittarius woman

He needs her beside him, but she needs the space to be by herself. She'll undoubtedly inflict a mortal wound when she asks why he's so dependent. But she'll bring him to the verge of suicide when he hands her a love poem and she laughs and shrieks, 'you've got to be kidding'.

She'll never understand his sensitivities, and he'll never understand her need for freedom. He'll become so infatuated with her vitality and sense of humour that he'll want to follow her to the supermarket and spend time with her while she stands in line. He'll get emotional over the way she butters her scones, and when she's not looking he'll fondle her tennis racket. Much of the time he spends with her he'll spend sulking in conspicuous silence, feverishly hoping that she's eating her heart out. However, she'll just slap him on the back cheerfully and ask if he has indigestion. All hope is lost, and he suddenly decides he wants to go home.

Cancer man with Capricorn woman

She'll be touched by the way he seems to care for her welfare, but she'll have a hard time dealing with his moods.

He seems to create slights and then sulk about them. No matter how hard she tries, she can never discover what she's done wrong. He'll resent all the time she spends at the office, not to mention the cocktail parties that seem to enhance business.

In turn, she'll resent his suspicions and the way he makes her feel guilty when she tries to ignore him. If she can manage to look at him from a less superficial standpoint, she may find a man who is very much worthy of her attentions. However, she'll have to pay in kind for his sympathy and services.

Cancer man with Aquarius woman

He creates closeness, but she feels more comfortable at a distance. He prefers cosy tête-à-têtes, while she embraces crowded scenes. He enjoys quiet evenings at home; she prefers mass riots. The differences between these two can be awesome: he needs a woman who will nurture his strength and overlook his insecurities; she needs a man who has fewer insecurities and a greater degree of emotional detachment.

Since she's adaptable to most personalities, she could come to love his. However, if he drowns her in a swamp of emotions and makes too many demands, she'll leave him to his sentimental dreams and memories of an affair that might have been.

Cancer man with Pisces woman

The psychic rapport between these two will leave him starry-eyed. He will sympathize with her mood swings, cry along with her during a weepy old movie and remember what she wore on the day he first met her. She'll marvel that he is a better cook than she is, is equally sensitive, and seems to know not only what she's thinking, but why.

They'll find themselves saying the same things simultaneously; they'll finish each other's sentences and respect each other's ideas. This relationship is made for lazy summer weekends by the sea and evenings with champagne and candlelight.

Monthly and Daily Guides

JANUARY

THE SUN WILL BE DRIFTING ALONG in the earthy sign of Capricorn until 20 January. That, of course, is your opposite sign, and so you seem to be concentrating a good deal on partnership affairs, both professional and personal. Mercury is in the same position as the Sun until the 11th, so there are minor changes taking place in all relationships. Luckily, you're not simply being drawn to people for their physical attributes: you also want to know what they think and what makes them tick. Therefore, you should learn a great deal.

Venus will be moving into Pisces on the 4th, where it stays for the remainder of the month, so for some of you there will be an attraction to a person who comes from a very different background, or perhaps someone who is involved in further education. Either way, life seems to be very interesting and fulfilling.

Fiery Mars will be drifting along in the water sign of Scorpio. This will certainly ginger up family life if you happen to have children; if you are fancy-free then you may be strongly attracted to throwing caution to the wind and seriously pursuing a hectic social life. Sports are well starred too because of the placing of this fiery planet.

Do remember that Pluto is in Sagittarius, and that this means you should eat more sensibly, otherwise you're likely to suffer from physical blockages: constipation is something frequently found amongst members of this sign.

The pattern the stars make this month suggests that you won't altogether have the reins of control in your own hands: it appears that other people will be influencing you more than usual, and that is saying quite a lot. However, it looks as if others do have your best interests at heart, so sift through the knowledge that comes your way and make your own decisions. Don't allow yourself to be swayed, because to keep chopping and changing will not help you to be efficient and successful.

Now look at the *Daily Guides* for further information.

1 MONDAY The day ahead will be emotional and outgoing but never boring. Money will flow in slowly at first, then faster as the days progress. Romance will be more important than usual; the Moon is in the watery sign of Pisces, so if you have somebody abroad then you're likely to be hearing from them.

2 TUESDAY Today Mars is in a difficult aspect with Neptune, so where work matters are concerned confusion seems to reign. Other people may be absent-minded and completely forget any promises they have made to you, and it's up to you to gently pull them down to earth and remind them of their obligations.

3 **WEDNESDAY** Today you might be dithering around, not clear on how to sort out one or two financial matters. You're worrying more than necessary at the moment. Just save your cash for a couple of weeks and delay making major commitments or purchases until you see how the land lies. It could be changeable in the near future, and you will need to reserve your judgement for the time being.

4 **THURSDAY** Today Venus will be moving into the watery sign of Pisces. That's the area of your chart devoted to foreign affairs and higher education, both of which seem to have a rosy glow over them. It's quite possible that you may be drawn to people with exciting foreign names, or somebody who is a little bit different from your usual type. You're certainly being adventurous over the next few weeks or so.

5 **FRIDAY** Today the Sun is lining up with Pluto, and the Sun, of course, is your financial planet, so it won't be at all surprising if this 24-hour period tends to block you in some way where finances are concerned. The best thing you can do is to shelve decisions until this day is out, find a better day and then push ahead.

6 **SATURDAY** Today the stars are likely to make you pause for thought more than in the past. What you truly want now is not what you wanted even a year ago, so be prepared to abandon what is no longer relevant. Being the tenacious character you are, you dislike change unless you've instigated it, but believe it or not what happens today will, later on, prove to be to your own benefit.

7   SUNDAY The faster you run today, the less far you seem to be getting. You can get so bogged down with emotional matters that you cannot see the proverbial wood for the trees. Do try to keep a firm game plan, and just chuck out what you dislike doing. Forcing yourself to do things which may be losing their attraction is really no good at all.

8   MONDAY If you feel short of friends, or think the future looks like an uphill slog, just consider that Saturn is around in Taurus sorting out the wheat from the chaff. You may be losing fair-weather friends and being encouraged to make a sensible plan for the long term, which may take a good deal of effort, but it will be rewarding in the end.

9   TUESDAY Today is the day of the full Moon, and unfortunately it falls in your sign. You'll walk into the room in one mood and walk out again almost a totally different person. No wonder other people are confused. The best thing you can do during this 24-hour period is to put the finishing touches to situations, jobs and work; having done that, you'll feel virtuous and will be raring to get back into life once more.

10   WEDNESDAY Mercury is about to move into the airy sign of Aquarius; that's the area of your chart devoted to people you are financially dependent upon, and it's quite likely that they'll want to make one or two changes during the next couple of weeks. Don't allow the word 'change' to fill you with dread: remember that many of the new phases we start in life can be exciting and productive, and that could very well be the case with this one.

11   THURSDAY If you want a day for making changes in your home, this is an ideal time. However, do not expect a quiet life. There will be much activity and telephone calls, and the hours will speed past. This is just the kind of day you thrive on. Decisions connected with those to whom you are closest can be taken with confidence.

12   FRIDAY What you want is to be indulged. What you have got are extra demands on your time, energy and patience. Everyone is looking up to you as the responsible one who needs to make the long-term decisions. Duty calls, so you will need to stick to the straight and narrow, at least during the daylight hours.

13   SATURDAY Today the Moon will be in the earthy sign of Virgo, and this may be pulling you back into your shell for a couple of days – emotionally at least. Let everyone race around following their own agendas and routines. You are struggling with serious thoughts and need to sort out your thinking. There are heavy pressures on you at this moment, but it's nothing that you cannot cope with.

14   SUNDAY Today Mercury is in a beautiful aspect with Neptune. This will most certainly be gingering up your imagination: therefore, if you work on anything at all creative or artistic you'll be putting a great deal of energy into what you are doing and will be soon receiving good results. This evening you're at your most romantic and gentle, so pick your company carefully.

15 MONDAY Today the Sun is lining up with Saturn, and because of this the people who are closest to you, both at work and at home, are confident, humorous and ready to do favours. Therefore, if you've been trying to pick the right time in order to make somebody see the truth, or perhaps to ask for any kind of support, then it has finally arrived. This evening could be a cuddly and an affectionate time.

16 TUESDAY Financially and emotionally you are feeling rather insecure, as if your world were not quite as generous a place as it once was. That is only a temporary mood, believe me. The truth is that you are learning lessons about self-sufficiency and independence which will prove to be very valuable in the future.

17 WEDNESDAY Today Mars is in a difficult aspect with Pluto, and this could create a certain amount of upheaval where your social plans are concerned. It might be a good idea during the day to double-check with people you are hoping to meet in the evening, just in case they have forgotten or changed their minds. Hopefully this is not the case, because you would be extremely disappointed.

18 THURSDAY There are heavier demands on your time at the moment, and a lot is being expected of you at work. You do not take criticism or negative comments well. However, sometimes they come from people whose judgement you trust, and these might be worth taking on board. If one close relationship feels rather cool and aloof, you will need to have a good deal of patience.

19 FRIDAY Listen to your body and see if you cannot adjust your lifestyle to suit your physical needs a good deal better. All the water signs have a tendency to become bogged down in emotions and also are inclined to think that they can keep going endlessly without pausing to recharge their batteries. Take the hint from the stars today and realize you are not superhuman, however nice that would be.

20 SATURDAY Saturn has a way of pointing out where you need to get your life better organized. Usually this means a good deal more work, but oddly enough this focus is now on your social and romantic relationships. Maybe you do have to push yourself harder or put in more effort to keep the kind of satisfying relationships that you are looking for.

21 SUNDAY Today the Sun will be moving into the airy sign of Aquarius; therefore, finances may be a little bit up and down during the coming month, but as you are a sensible person you should be able to balance the books. Furthermore, people you are financially dependent upon will be a good deal more sunny, optimistic and positive, so it might be a good time to ask for any kind of favour or tip.

22 MONDAY Force yourself to get a grip of practical details first thing in the morning. Reality is not your strong point, as you are a rather creative, dreamy sign, but you know from the attitude of workmates or everyday companions that you do need to streamline your efficiency.

23 TUESDAY Friends or loved ones may be in a fighting mood, but the minute you start to fight back you'll win hands down. A buoyant mood is reflected in your ability to strike one or two profitable deals, and soon the aspects will show you at your most innovative and daring. But know when to stop.

24 WEDNESDAY Today is the day of the new Moon, and it falls in the sign of Aquarius. New Moons always make you feel more optimistic and ready to get into the fray and get exactly what you want out of life. This is a great time for new beginnings in your professional or personal life, so push ahead, and be open-minded to new faces that you might meet.

25 THURSDAY Today Jupiter finally resumes direct movement, so the frustration and delays you might recently have met with, particularly at work, will slowly begin to melt away as the days go by. You're beginning to feel as if you are on top of the world, and that's exactly where you can be.

26 FRIDAY Today Saturn resumes direct movement too. Therefore, the complications that have been wrought by other people slowly begin to fade. Your relationships, both at work and at home, are on the up and up, and anyone new you meet during the next couple of weeks is likely to be important.

27 SATURDAY Deal with ongoing commitments swiftly over the next few days, and get them out of the way. The stars' influence is about to help you to break down barriers which, up until now, have stopped you from feeling that you are part of a very special group, set or organization. Today's stars should make you grin from ear to ear.

28 SUNDAY Hidden fears about work or money are coming to the surface, but self-doubt should be dealt with once and for all. Rumour may have it that your progress will be so rapid that you're leaving others behind. The planets are encouraging you to make it clear that, wherever you go, your loved ones go with you.

29 MONDAY Refuse to be drawn into a tug-of-war between work and family. Save your energy for surprise developments, which – under the stars' influence – will put your creativity to the test. Soon the stars will offer a perfect opportunity to show off the talents you have left untapped. Soon after, the planets will provide a one-way ticket to Paradise.

30 TUESDAY Petty politics must be ignored, as you anticipate giant strides being made with regard to money, property or the family. You'll soon realize you are one of life's leaders, not one of the followers, and

someone close will find you more appealing and
impressive than ever. Listen to what is whispered in
your ear, because to overlook it could mean you'll
miss out.

31 WEDNESDAY The feeling that other people may be
competing for your love or affection must not be allowed
to disrupt your day. The stars are making links which
suggest you have a lot more power and influence than
you realize. Over the next few days your thoughts and
observations will put you ahead of the game.

FEBRUARY

THE SUN THIS MONTH will continue to coast along in the
airy sign of Aquarius up until the 19th. This is the area of
your chart devoted to people you are financially dependent
upon, and they seem to be having a good time. Even so, a pat
on the back from you will probably lead to them girding their
loins and doing even better, so make sure that you supply it.

From the 20th the Sun will be coasting along in the
water sign of Pisces, highlighting matters related to further
education and foreign countries. If you have someone
important at a distance, you are likely to be hearing from
them more than once during this period. Furthermore, it's an
excellent time for learning anything new or attempting to
pass tests or examinations; if this rings a bell with you, you're
likely to be doing well, but don't get overconfident.

For the majority of the month Mercury will be sailing
along in the airy sign of Aquarius, the Water Bearer. This

suggests that you are likely to be becoming more positive and, perhaps, adventurous. Friends and acquaintances will be popping in and out of your life at this time, and you will need to keep a grip on things to avoid becoming confused.

Venus will be situated in fiery Aries from the 3rd onwards. This is the zenith point of your chart, and because of this it's quite likely that you may become romantically involved with somebody you meet either at work or whilst going about your everyday business. If you have a mate at home, you will need to control this urge, because lust is no replacement for somebody who really cares about you. Furthermore, if you are in an artistic job, you're going to be shining during the next few weeks and gleaning all of the praise.

Mars begins its journey through the fiery sign of Sagittarius on the 15th. Therefore, be especially watchful where health matters are concerned, because you are prone to accidents, particularly when in the kitchen, bathroom, or anywhere where you can find hot objects. As long as you slow down and take care in these areas, there's no reason at all why you shouldn't emerge from February hale and hearty. Lastly, if you wish to approach people in positions of authority, such as your boss or your bank manager, then you will need to use a certain amount of charm. If you're too pushy, I'm afraid you could be making trouble for yourself.

The pattern the stars make this month seems to suggest that whatever happens during February will be a result, directly or indirectly, of your own actions. Therefore, there's no point in blaming anybody else if things go wrong: take that responsibility, use it well, and you will have a productive time.

Now look at the *Daily Guides* for further information.

1 **THURSDAY** Money matters are not nearly as crucial and important as they seem, especially in the light of what comes to you by way of a partner or loved one. Although the day seems fairly ordinary at the beginning, there is mystery and expectancy in the air. You'll know why very soon: in the meantime I'm afraid you'll just have to be patient.

2 **FRIDAY** Put your heart and soul into a partnership or romance as soon as possible, as quite different demands will soon dominate. Twice within the next few days there are interesting aspects which will empower you to transform your work or daily routine into something more pleasing and profitable. If a loved one feels resentful or left out, you can provide proof that you're doing the right thing.

3 **SATURDAY** Today Venus will be moving to the zenith point of your chart, throwing a happy, harmonious glow over work affairs, particularly if you happen to be creative or artistic. Furthermore, many of you will become romantically involved with someone you meet through professional duties, and while the romance may not last for ever, it'll do for quite a considerable time.

4 **SUNDAY** Today Mercury decides to go into retrograde action, so from hereon in paperwork, travelling and legal matters could all be unduly complicated. Where possible, shelve them until this state of affairs is rectified, because failure to do so will be storing up a good deal of aggravation for yourself.

5   MONDAY A sudden change of plan requires you to come to somebody's rescue, but what you are made to sacrifice will be replaced many times over. The stars right now will attract a number of new fans or admirers. Don't let the flattery force you to forget who you are and where you came from.

6   TUESDAY Shrug off any tiffs, tears or tantrums, and act on an instinct that gives early warning of some basic changes on the home and family front. Even more significant should be the news relating to your work or finances, which is emphasized by a little cosmic magic occurring in your birth chart. Save your energy: you'll need every spare ounce very soon.

7   WEDNESDAY Mercury is now in retrograde action, and while this lasts it is important that you do not push ahead where travel or legal matters are concerned, because to do so would be making life unduly complicated for yourself. Furthermore, if you have a Gemini or Virgo in your life, then their moods are likely to vary, and this could prove to be very frustrating.

8   THURSDAY Today is the day of the full Moon and it occurs in the fiery sign of Leo. That is the area of your chart devoted to cash and possessions, so there's a strong chance that you may pay over the odds for some item or perhaps lose something important. Carry the minimum amount of possessions around with you and you'll help to offset this particular trend.

9   FRIDAY If a colleague or loved one appears to take advantage of you, let the stars inspire you to find a permanent solution. With so many good things being said about you, there's no need to settle for second best. In fact, over the next few days the stars will rid you of much that has held you back in the past. A major journey is about to begin.

10   SATURDAY Love and rivalry are on your mind, but the planets will soon provide bigger fish to fry. This could be a time during which you are feted, applauded and rewarded. Also, you can expect to see the culmination of exciting involvements begun a while ago. Planetary forces in your own sign mean that you should hear the words you've been waiting for.

11   SUNDAY Suddenly your ideas seem so expansive that you may be subjected to the scepticism of those who take a safe, sure direction in life. Although it's true that funds could present a problem with all that you want to do, that alone is no reason to give up hope. You have a great deal going for you: remember it.

12   MONDAY It wouldn't be fair to ask you to choose between family and work commitments, but there are times like this when, through a clash of interests, your loyalties are divided. Make an unsentimental decision about what must be pursued and what you can ignore, and don't alter it, whatever happens.

13   TUESDAY A badly timed argument has a lot to do with someone's concerns over money. But there are enough people close by to provide what you need until the situation improves, which it will soon. The stars right now remind you that pride can be a serious handicap. No-one can afford to let it do its worst.

14 WEDNESDAY Even though others may think your attitude self-indulgent, you know that hidden benefits are often provided by pursuing what might appear to be a frivolous pastime or involvement. Let the stars' influence help you prove how much can be gained if you have total trust in what you're doing.

15 THURSDAY Today that fiery planet, Mars, will be moving into the fiery sign of Sagittarius. This area of your chart is devoted to people you are financially dependent upon, whether that is your mate or perhaps your boss. Such people are in for a hectic, hard-working time and may run out of patience on occasions, which you should not take too seriously. Be as supportive and as kind as you can, and let them know that you are there for them: it will help.

16 FRIDAY The fact that you feel fonder than ever for a particular person doesn't mean there are no aspects of this relationship that leave you upset or angry. Every confident planet is urging you to take time and trouble to deal with areas which you tend to gloss over. The flaws will disappear sooner than you think.

17 SATURDAY Heated discussions over money will turn out to be little more than a lot of hot air. You can improve the atmosphere by introducing an idea you know will leave family and loved ones a lot better off. But don't give the game away too soon. Your news deserves the best possible hearing.

18 SUNDAY Although a loved one may not agree with the ways you spend your money or your time, you're drawn towards the type of work or area of responsibility you know will bring rewards. Even though you might not gain a great deal financially, you will end up very much in profit in terms of knowledge.

19 MONDAY The Sun is about to move into the watery sign of Pisces, and this is the area of your chart devoted to higher education, long-distance travel, foreign affairs and legal matters. All of these sides to life are likely to be lucky for you, so it is important that you push ahead with them with as much confidence as you can muster. See what you can do.

20 TUESDAY Perhaps you have been exposed to family upheavals recently. As a result, you've learnt a lot about human nature and might look back on this as a very informative period in your life. You've also gleaned valuable insights into your own behaviour patterns. Used well, these could provide a useful strategy for the future.

21 WEDNESDAY Any slip-up at home or work can be forgotten, as your track record shows you up in a good light. You, of course, like to think of yourself as infallible, and a blow to your pride is punishment enough for any error made. But you can spend your

time and energy in far better ways than giving yourself a
hard time.

22 THURSDAY Your conscientious nature prevents you
from letting standards slip. But somebody is taking
advantage of you at a time when you'd like to put your
personal affairs before everything else. You needn't be
blunt or aggressive: a subtle reminder of what you've
achieved will do the trick.

23 FRIDAY Today is the day of the new Moon, so you
should be in tip-top form. New Moons always fill you
with optimism and provide you with a chance for
starting again, and this one is no exception. The fact
that it happens to be falling in Pisces suggests that if you
have people abroad they will be getting in touch. If
you're taking any kind of test or examination, you will
do well, so don't worry.

24 SATURDAY If recent successes have met with less
applause than you had envisaged, remember that not
everyone shares your generosity of spirit or sense of fair
play. Of course, your enthusiasm won't be dampened,
and you may soon be making even greater efforts to
stride ahead. Those left behind have only themselves
to blame.

25 SUNDAY Finally Mercury resumes direct movement,
so from hereon in you will find precious little danger in
connection with long-distance travelling, legal matters or
paperwork. In fact, these are the very areas that you
should push like crazy, as they're sure to be lucky for you.

26 MONDAY Disappointing news may emerge from an unreliable source, and it mustn't stop you from going ahead with plans made some while ago. You have a great wealth of knowledge, which those in authority will one day be happy to pay for. Don't let your zeal and enthusiasm dwindle as a result of rumour or hearsay.

27 TUESDAY Now that you're close to overtaking those who had led the field, you should feel grateful that you've pushed yourself so hard and that a valuable prize you had never dreamed of winning could be yours. You have made a great impression, rest assured.

28 WEDNESDAY You may not like to appear obsessed with money, but you can't afford to be seen as a soft touch, especially by those keen to pool resources with you over a deal. A clash between the planets right now shows that this could be a time when you must bare your teeth.

MARCH

THIS MONTH THE SUN will be coasting along in the watery sign of Pisces up until the 20th. That's the area of your chart devoted to matters related to abroad, to legal matters, and also to adventure in general. If you're trying to book a holiday for the summer, you are sure to get good value at the moment.

From the 21st onwards, the Sun will be moving through

fiery Aries. That is the zenith point of your chart, and you begin one of the most hard-working periods of this year. Of course, you are not at all averse to hard work: you can pull out all the stops to equal anybody else. However, it wouldn't be a good idea to concentrate completely on professional matters when your personal life seems to be in something of a flux. Distribute your energies evenly and you'll have a good time.

Mercury will continue its journey through Aquarius up until the 17th. During this time, the people you are financially dependent upon will want to make changes. You must at least be open-minded to what they have to say, because when you have had sufficient time to think things through you'll realize they know exactly what they are doing.

On the 18th Mercury will be moving into the water sign of Pisces. Therefore, if you have anybody abroad you'll be receiving some gossip in connection with them; furthermore, you should be successful in any test or examination you take, but don't become overconfident.

Venus is in Aries, the zenith point of your chart, so you'll be combining business with pleasure and perhaps love, too, more than usual. You must take care though, because Venus will be going into retrograde movement on the 10th, and when this happens you could find yourself lumbered with an unsatisfactory relationship where somebody is playing you off against somebody else, and you're not the sort of person who can cope with this.

Mars continues its journey through fiery Sagittarius, making for a certain amount of stress in the people you are closest to, especially if you are financially dependent upon them. Give them your backing and encouragement: it makes all the difference. This is a month for being as supportive as you possibly can, and if you put others before yourself you'll certainly be glad you did in a couple of months or so.

The pattern the planets make during March suggests that, for the most part, you have the reins of control in your own hands. Consequently, if anything goes wrong, there's no point in blaming anybody but yourself. Still, it's always nice to know that we are in a position to make choices; just make sure that you think yours through before you set them in concrete. That way, you shouldn't have much to regret.

Now look at the *Daily Guides* for further information.

1   THURSDAY Anyone who says your plans are overambitious might have to eat their words at some point soon. True, the planetary setup may mean you've got too much to say for yourself, but it also suggests you'll be bringing to the surface resources that you have been unaware of; you may surprise those closest to you and maybe even yourself.

2   FRIDAY Since it seems you're about to accumulate some money or material possessions, you may feel more secure during the next few months than you have for quite some time. The planets will also be encouraging you to share your feelings of wellbeing with those closest to you. When under stress and strain, we all tend to underestimate the strength and power that certain relationships can provide. Make a habit of saying 'thank you'.

3   SATURDAY Encouraged as you should be by the overall reaction to your latest ideas, you might be happy to collude with someone who has similar objectives in mind. Even so, you must safeguard yourself against the possibility of having your thunder stolen from you. Insist you're given whatever credit is due.

4 SUNDAY The Moon is in the airy sign of Gemini, and that's a rather secretive part of your chart. Because of this you may be feeling uncomfortable without any clear reason. Obviously then, it isn't a good time to tackle anything or anyone important; simply let the day drift on while you potter about and keep that busy mind active.

5 MONDAY It might be worth thinking about teaming up with someone in a financial or professional capacity, but make sure that any deals work for, not against you. It's possible that you have overlooked a grey area that could affect your reputation. If in doubt, seek expert advice.

6 TUESDAY Today the Sun is in a difficult aspect with Pluto, and you may feel that you are blocked, particularly where finances are concerned. The best thing you can do is to make your plans, but wait for a better day before leaping into action, because to do so now is surely a mistake.

7 WEDNESDAY Not everyone can see why you are so conscientious with regard to work or family duties. But you know you're investing in something which constantly yields dividends. Developments over the next few days will make you so proud of your achievements that it will be impossible not to let your feelings show.

8 **THURSDAY** The feedback from family or loved ones indicates that you have made wise choices and come up with some very popular schemes. The knock-on effect this has on your health and wellbeing will mean that you feel so strong and able that you continue to produce better and better ideas all the time.

9 **FRIDAY** Today is the day of the full Moon, and it occurs in the earthy sign of Virgo. This is the area of your chart devoted to short trips and to the mind. I'm afraid there could be a certain amount of disappointment that you may have to cope with. Never mind: if you are sensible and use this day for putting finishing touches to conversations, phone calls and work in general, you'll be using it in the most profitable way.

10 **SATURDAY** Today Venus goes into retrograde movement. While this state of affairs exists, it would not be a good idea for you to turn your attention to property matters or family problems. Emotional affairs could be a little bit touchy, so remember that other people have sensitive feelings too: you're not alone in feeling lost, abandoned and disappointed on occasions. Selflessness is the key word.

11 **SUNDAY** You may feel flattered at being asked to join some group or gathering. It hasn't occurred to you that your presence means a great deal, and that you shouldn't feel grateful for the fact that you've been included. At times like this your modesty may be appealing, but it does mean you tend to undersell yourself: don't let this occur.

12 MONDAY A speech, announcement or notice is about to alter the way you see yourself with regard to your work or finances. True, there's nothing dramatic implied, but with the planetary setup today suggesting this could lead to bigger changes later on, you should feel optimistic. All eyes might soon be on you, so make sure you look your best.

13 TUESDAY Perhaps a move into unfamiliar territory seems daunting, but you may be sure of being given a warm welcome and a great deal of help. You're still imagining that someone is working to a hidden agenda, but you should stop being so sceptical and accept what you're being offered at face value. Everything seems to be fine.

14 WEDNESDAY If a special relationship is showing signs of wear and tear, you might do well to introduce an element of surprise, perhaps involving travel or an intriguing get-together. The planets are currently pulling you in a direction that you don't normally take. Perhaps it's about time that you did something daring and different.

15 THURSDAY Today the Sun is lining up with Pluto, so where finances are concerned you may be well and truly blocked, or perhaps act out of character and do something foolish. Think twice before digging deeply into your bank account, because you could live to regret it in quite a big way.

16 FRIDAY Today the Sun is lining up with Saturn, and consequently there's a serious, down-to-earth feel about this particular day, especially where partnerships are concerned. You are no longer prepared to fool yourself into believing this is it, and the person concerned could be feeling shocked by your positive attitude. However, it won't do you any harm to seem a bit more aggressive.

17 SATURDAY Mercury is about to move into the watery sign of Pisces, and that's the area of your chart devoted to higher education and foreign affairs. It's likely that you are suffering from itchy feet and will be rushing out to buy a holiday, in which case you'll probably get good value for money.

18 SUNDAY You seem to be a little bit too perfectionist in your personal life. Unless you can honestly say with your hand on your heart that you are perfect yourself, you have no right to expect this from other people.

19 MONDAY Today Mars is lining up with Pluto, and so there's a rather explosive feel about this time. It won't be a good idea for you to come on too strong with people you hardly know, or you'll easily give offence without meaning to. A work project may be blocked too, but as long as you can remain patient and be your normal cautious self, you will take this in your stride and rearrange your timetable.

20 TUESDAY A long overdue chat could mean you'll be embarking on something which will give your everyday life the boost it needs. So don't let your conscience insist you remain on a treadmill, which will still turn, even though you may be a distance away. Your contribution is invaluable but not indispensable.

21 WEDNESDAY The Sun is moving into the fiery sign of Aries. That is the zenith point of your chart, and therefore you begin a hard-working period. The best thing to do is to make a few sensible plans before you move in any one direction; you don't want to have to backtrack at a later date, because you'd only become impatient with yourself, not to mention other people.

22 THURSDAY What begins as a casual liaison may take on greater significance. But although it would be nice to believe what you're being told, you mustn't get carried away with an idea which, in truth, sounds fairly impractical. Enjoy what you have without trying to transform it into something it can never be.

23 FRIDAY Someone's lack of consideration could make you reluctant to be your usual helpful self. However, the planets' influence is sure to remind you how uneasy a guilty conscience can make you feel. You know you'll do the right thing. But perhaps you should just add one or two words of warning for next time.

24 SATURDAY Once again you're being reminded how your mood can alter when someone comes up with the words you want to hear. Although some of it may need to be taken with a pinch of salt, you're about to be flattered into believing you're a very special person indeed. You are, but beware.

25 SUNDAY Today is the day of the new Moon, and it occurs in the fiery sign of Aries, the zenith point of your chart. It's unlikely that you'll get through the next couple of days without some minor new beginning on the professional front. As always with you, the Moon, whether full or new, affects you quite considerably, but a new one like this should put you in high spirits. Therefore, if you want to approach a member of the opposite sex, then do feel free to do just that.

26 MONDAY The day ahead will be a confident one, but not always clear in its direction. Friends will be confusing and will not always be there when you want them to be, so you must be focussed. There's a strong chance, too, that your financial situation will suddenly improve dramatically.

27 TUESDAY You start this day on top form, with almost everything you touch turning to gold, so do not lose that good humour when a situation blows up later. You're spending like mad, then having to pacify partners who feel they should have a say in what you buy. Be cool, be calm, and be good to yourself.

28 WEDNESDAY The planets today make you a model of diplomacy and sugary charm. You wish you could say the same for one close companion who is dancing around like a cat on a hot tin roof. If you can find time for yourself, you will sail along quite happily, but it is a fine balance to strike.

29 THURSDAY Today the Sun will be lining up with Neptune, and as a result there may be a chance for you to gain through something creative or artistic. However, you mustn't allow this to make you believe that you can spend more than you can realistically afford. Self-deception can be your worst enemy; make sure that it isn't on this particular day.

30 FRIDAY Your efforts are beginning to bear fruit, and you find that recognition for your talents is rolling in. Resting on your laurels is not an option, but it is more pleasant to apply yourself when you know success is assured. Your popularity among the right people is keeping your diary full.

31 SATURDAY No-one can turn on the charm quite like you when you put your mind to it, and, of course, when you're in the mood. You are laying on the seductive persuasion now, which is having a wonderful effect on everybody. Conceal irritations, and flash a winning smile. You may not be feeling cooperative, but there is no sense in letting that show.

APRIL

THIS MONTH THE SUN will be coasting along in the fiery sign of Aries up until the 20th, and that is the area of your chart devoted to work and status. No longer will you be prepared to take a back seat: you want the limelight, and you want it bad. Anybody who stands in the way may realize that underneath your soft exterior there's an essential hardness which you're prepared to use if it is absolutely necessary.

On the 21st the Sun will be moving into the earthy sign of Taurus, and that is the aspect of your chart connected with friends and acquaintances, so you seem to be in demand at this time. New people will appear in your scene who are likely to be important to you, either because they are only too willing to help you out with your ambitions, or perhaps because there is a romantic interest here. Be your usual cautious self, and you'll get through this month gleaning a certain amount of satisfaction as well as reward.

Mercury this month will be situated in Pisces during the first week. That's the area of your chart devoted to long-distance travelling, foreign affairs and legal matters, all of which can be pushed happily. Furthermore, Mercury suggests that you can sign all paperwork without fearing there may be a gigantic pitfall for you to fall into.

From the 7th onwards, Mercury will be moving through the fiery sign of Aries. That's the rather secretive area of your chart, which means there's a good deal going on behind the scenes, and particularly where finances are concerned it is necessary for you to keep your fingers on the pulse. Your imagination is running riot too, and if you need this for your job, you will be doing exceptionally well.

Venus is still in the fiery sign of Aries, the zenith point of your chart. Therefore, it seems that the trend to be attracted to people you meet through your job will continue for a good deal longer. Those in creative jobs will be doing exceptionally well and receiving several pats on the back, congratulations, and maybe even a celebration. There seems to be a great deal of goodwill and opportunity where work matters are concerned, and it's up to you to recognize and make the most of them.

Mars continues its long journey through the fiery sign of Sagittarius. Consequently, the people that you are financially dependent upon are still sure to be having something of a difficult ride. Whatever you do, don't criticize or put them down; instead, make sure that you are there for them whenever life gets a bit too tough. In this way they will be able to return to the fray refreshed and ready to make the most of any opportunity that comes along.

The pattern the stars make this month seems to suggest that you continue to have the reins of your life in your control. Therefore, if anything goes wrong, it won't be fair of you to put the blame on somebody else: accept the fact that you have made a mistake, and see what you can do to rescue the situation. This can easily be done with a little bit of imagination, not to mention your splendid tenacity.

Now look at the *Daily Guides* for further information.

1   SUNDAY It's quite likely that the stars may make you feel pressured, discouraged and rather brittle, but when it comes to turning up trumps, as it is now, you feel a surge of power. You know your influence is spreading, partly because you are right, and partly because you have a wonderful way with words and charm. However, do watch your spending.

2   MONDAY You are coming on a bit strong and making close partners jumpy. They're trying to soothe and smooth things in your wake, but maybe you have said enough to bring tensions into the open. However, make sure you do not upset those you basically like by saying too much. This can easily happen, you know.

3 TUESDAY The planets right now are rather indulgent, but this will not be too much of a worry for you, since you burn up energy at a rate of knots. However, perhaps you need to work out better rules for your relationships. This is helpful, since it helps to iron out problems before they begin to appear.

4 WEDNESDAY Fired with enthusiasm as you are today, you are likely to be rushing around, secretly pulling out all the stops to ensure easier days ahead. Maybe the time has come to stop putting yourself down and realize that you are a richer, stronger personality than you ever give yourself credit for. Friends give a real boost, and loved ones are in a romantic mood.

5 THURSDAY Jupiter is in a beautiful aspect with Neptune, so you should be doing well where matters related to abroad, legal affairs and your aspirations are concerned. This evening it won't take much to set your heart a-flutter; therefore, use a bit of common sense before you throw yourself in feet first.

6 FRIDAY Suddenly you see an answer or a solution to long-term worries. You're speaking your mind and not allowing anything to dampen your spirits. Just don't go laying down the law with loved ones: they're aiming for a quiet few days, while you seem to be on all systems go. Live and let live is your best motto for the present.

7 SATURDAY Today Mercury will be moving into Aries, and that is the zenith point of your chart. Therefore, if you are asked to take any kind of trip for the sake of professional matters, you should accept, because it'll be good for you. Paperwork, too, seems to be important, and if you are signing contracts you'll be doing well. Legal affairs can be pushed too.

8 SUNDAY This is the day of the full Moon, and it occurs in the airy sign of Libra, the area of your chart devoted to family and property. Either could be a source of complication for a couple of days: you'll need to hold on to your patience, sit down sensibly and talk matters through with loved ones before making a move, otherwise you could make a mistake.

9 MONDAY It seems that you will definitely get a particular money matter sorted out, which will bring a smile to your face. You want more control, influence and status, and getting your finances into better shape is part of your strategy. Your opinions are loud and strong, but remember persuasion works better if you tread more softly.

10 TUESDAY Your assumption that someone you esteem highly is aware of your true feelings could be the cause of current confusion. You may think you are showing your caring, considerate side, but perhaps it's being interpreted as condescending. You're too far down the line to play charades. Try a direct approach instead.

11 WEDNESDAY In trying to appear nonchalant, you'll make matters worse for those who realize you're experiencing some sort of confusion or torment. Even though confidentiality is an issue, you can surely share at least half the burden with someone you trust. You're not the only one who can keep a secret, you know.

12 THURSDAY Now that the heat has gone out of a situation which could have affected your work or reputation, you can turn your attention to more pleasing issues. In doing so, you'll realize that much of the joy you gain from a close relationship stems from the fact that it's virtually maintenance free. Don't take it for granted.

13 FRIDAY A chance to indulge in some sort of escapist activity may relieve tension as pressure builds up in different areas. That's fine, so long as you know the point at which you're in danger of appearing irresponsible or uncaring. Remember how hard you had to work for what you have now. Guard it carefully.

14 SATURDAY Today Mercury is in a fine aspect with Pluto, so although you may change your mind about several important matters, it looks as if this is the right thing to do. Perhaps you haven't considered every eventuality, in which case Pluto will be helping you to clear out the confusion from your brain and begin to think a bit more clearly.

15 SUNDAY Someone making a fuss over something that would normally be brushed aside may fall foul of criticism from those less understanding than you. But you're aware that there are hidden factors at work and a sympathetic approach will achieve far more than a telling-off. Prove your point whenever you're ready.

16 MONDAY The need to appraise a proposal or business opportunity is weighing more heavily than it should. Don't make the mistake of letting sentiment come into a decision-making process which is about hard cash and little else. If the figures add up on paper, they will do so in practice. If not, don't go any further.

17 TUESDAY Everything points to the fact that you're achieving great things, but you seem reluctant to show that you're pleased. With the stars at a crucial point, your insecurities are emphasized. Don't worry. In a day or two you'll be puffing out your chest with pride.

18 WEDNESDAY An offer or suggestion arriving out of the blue may not sound particularly exciting to some people, but you're the only one who knows the circumstances involved. You realize there are factors other than money to consider if you are to reap the rewards you most want. A sense of balance is essential.

19 THURSDAY Today Mercury is lining up with Uranus, and so it's unlikely that you will get through the day without at least one change of mind. If you are really in doubt over something serious, it might be a good idea to wait until today's aspects have passed so that you can see things more clearly and confidently.

20 FRIDAY Today Venus decides to resume direct movement. Consequently, matters related to friends and acquaintances will run much more smoothly than they have of late. If you have fallen out with somebody, this is the ideal time for admitting that perhaps you both got things out of proportion.

21 SATURDAY Today Saturn will be moving into Gemini. Unfortunately, this is the rather secretive area of your chart, and also one that represents your subconscious, so you may find yourself thinking negatively and feeling defeated before you even begin. Hopefully, now you have read this, you will be able to shake off this attitude, step out into the world and grapple with it wherever necessary.

22 SUNDAY Today Mercury will be moving into the earthy sign of Taurus, so there'll be a series of events occurring in the lives of your friends. Furthermore, the inclination to spend money at clubs and on romance is increasing, but as long as you use that canny head of yours, you won't do too much damage.

23 MONDAY Today is the day of the new Moon, and it occurs in the earthy sign of Taurus. That's the area of your chart devoted to friends, and so it's unlikely you'll get through the day without becoming attracted to somebody who may be like-minded. Your friendship circle is certainly emphasized, so get out tonight, perhaps to a club, where you can get together with them.

24 TUESDAY What started out as a simple way of linking up with a few companions could escalate into a much larger gathering. Although it may be nice to include everyone in your plans, there are limits to the budget, if not to the time and energy it would take to organize a more elaborate get-together. Know when to say 'no'.

25 WEDNESDAY Certain ethical questions may create a divide between yourself and someone with whom you normally see eye to eye, and you must ensure that no lasting damage is done. The stars today are overemphasizing the importance of what has been said. Be the first to admit you spoke too soon.

26 THURSDAY Having learnt to juggle with finances and differentiate between what is needed and what is wanted, you should begin to feel that everything you have learnt over the past few months will stand you in good stead for the next important phase of your life. When something valuable, either in financial or emotional terms, lands in your lap, it won't alter your thinking on what's important and what's not. But it will mean there are good times ahead.

27 FRIDAY Until you allow yourself the luxury of making the odd mistake, you will not be able to relax and enjoy something which a loved one is keen to share with you. No-one is expecting you to excel in an area that's completely unknown to you, or to set new world records. An indication that you're keen to learn is all that is required.

28 SATURDAY Controversial topics may be discussed, and the fact that your views differ dramatically from those of a loved one should not be a cause for concern. Put the current changeable atmosphere down to the planets, and don't imagine you'll gain points for saying what's expected of you. Your conviction is what counts.

29 SUNDAY You're not afraid to fly in the face of convention at times, you may be well advised to cut your losses and quit rather than proceed with a current venture. Delay any longer and it's your money or time that could go to waste. Better to retrench, rethink and give yourself the chance to come up with something better.

30 MONDAY There's no point in talking endlessly about ambitious plans concerning your family or domestic environment. Unless you hurl yourself into action, you will soon find everyone has grown tired of listening to the same old story. No matter how good your intentions may be, they are going to waste. Act fast.

MAY

DURING THIS MONTH, the Sun will be drifting through the earthy sign of Taurus up until the 21st. That is the area of your chart devoted to friends, acquaintances and, to some extent, your ambitions. Group activities are well starred and will offer you plenty of chances for meeting new faces; some of these meetings can be turned around into romances, but whether you choose to do so is, of course, your decision.

There's a possibility, too, that you'll be bumping into many Taureans, and they'll turn out to be good, fast friends.

On the 22nd the Sun will be moving into the airy sign of Gemini, the portion of your chart devoted to what is going on behind the scenes, your imagination and your intuition. All of these can be utilized to swell your bank account and for solving problems, so listen to your gut feelings, because you're going to regret it if you don't.

Mercury remains in Taurus during the first week of May; therefore, if you need to go on business trips or sign important documents, this is the time to choose.

After the 7th, Mercury will be moving into Gemini. This will emphasize your intuitions, and it is important that you listen to them rather than making decisions on the spur of the moment. You may find it more difficult than usual to sleep. If it's hard to turn off your busy brain, make a hot bath and a warm drink, and this should solve the problem nicely.

Venus will be situated in Aries for the entire month, throwing a rosy and sociable glow over your circle of friends and acquaintances. Regardless of your own sex, it is female friends who are likely to be there for you, so don't feel that you are being weak or feeble-minded if you need a second opinion on anything important. Others will be only too glad to put in their two pennyworth, although whether you act on it will be entirely up to you. Socially, you're likely to be taking part in team activities or visiting clubs, and all in all you seem to have a great deal to look forward to on the leisure front this May.

Mars continues to plod on through Sagittarius: it's almost as if it has got stuck there. Therefore, the people you are financially dependent upon continue to be rather stressed out and in need of love and encouragement. You know how it feels to be out of step with the world: it happens to all of us from time to time. So make sure you show your compassionate side; others will be grateful to you for some time to come.

The pattern the stars make this month suggests that the emphasis is very much on the material side of life. There will be important decisions for you to make, and as long as you are as canny and shrewd as usual, you'll do the right thing at the right time.

Lastly, just a reminder to be a little bit more upfront where your emotions are concerned: there's no reason why May can't be one of the most enjoyable months of the year, but failure to follow this advice could wreck everything, leaving you stressed and totally confused.

Now look at the *Daily Guides* for further information.

1   TUESDAY Even though you may not have all the money you want, you have something which is enviable, marketable and potentially full of power. These things don't happen overnight, but the way you are perceived at this stage will persuade others to earmark you for bigger things. Smile: you're being watched.

2   WEDNESDAY On those occasions when you feel lost or nervous, no-one would ever know it. However, the stars are urging you to remind others that you are a human being, not a robot. It would do you no harm to admit that you sometimes go weak at the knees when the going gets tough. Indeed, you will be seen as a good deal stronger for it.

3   THURSDAY Stop waiting for a loved one to provide you with the excitement and inspiration you feel your life is lacking. Every now and again you have to break out of your mould and do something newsworthy, rash, or even reckless. And if that thought makes you feel as though you're on a white-knuckled ride, then enjoy it.

4   FRIDAY Through no fault of your own, you seem to have become involved in a network of intrigue or deceit. Now that a line can be drawn under this episode, honesty and trust will once more become an integral part of your day-to-day existence. Deal in the plain, simple truth, and insist that others do the same.

5   SATURDAY It seems that someone has made fundamental changes which could come up against a little resistance. You might be the one in the hot seat, as you're no doubt a great deal more decisive and astute than those around you. Put sentiment to one side. A Cancerian always knows when it is time to begin again.

6   SUNDAY If no-one else is going to sing your praises, you had better do it yourself. There are a number of things you want and need now that one cycle in your life has ended. Don't for one moment think you will be respected or admired for settling for less than you deserve. If you're unhappy, let someone know about it.

7   MONDAY Today is the day of the full Moon, and it occurs in the watery sign of Scorpio. Because of this it might be a good idea for you to double-check all your social and romantic arrangements, because something could go completely wrong. Furthermore, set aside artistic work for the time being, and wait for the full Moon to pass before you do anything important, otherwise you may have to retrace your steps.

8 TUESDAY Mercury has now moved into the airy sign of Gemini. That's the rather secretive part of your chart, so from hereon in you may be much more reserved than usual. For reasons best known to yourself, you want to keep a low profile: maybe you have a big decision to make and are wisely thinking twice before rushing in.

9 WEDNESDAY Having made a fuss about the way things should be, you cannot be seen to let the slightest opportunity go to waste. Those in authority have bowed to your wisdom as you seem to be the one who knows what's needed. If you appear ungrateful or ungracious, you'll lose a lot of power and respect.

10 THURSDAY Although you are right to focus on more pressing matters, you can now show that when circumstances work in your favour, you know how to have a good time. The stars urge you to forget your inhibitions and be guided by your passions. You'll create a stir, but at least you won't be overlooked or left out.

11 FRIDAY Today Mars moves into retrograde action. This means you could be in for a certain amount of frustration where professional matters are concerned. It's going to seem to you that you're taking three steps

back for every step forward, but if you can weather the
storm in your usual tenacious way, you will triumph.

12 SATURDAY Today Mercury is lining up with
Neptune, and so there's a creative, but confusing, feel
about this particular day. If you work in a creative job,
you'll be doing exceptionally well, but you're in danger
of skipping over something important, such as boring
routine. Life cannot always be full of highs: there are
times when everything goes along on an even keel, and
this is one of them.

13 SUNDAY Before you start resenting monotony or
routine, ask yourself whether you have been slow in
following up opportunities concerning your work or
social standing. Anyone can complain about drawing of
the short straw, but you can improve the situation
dramatically if you try.

14 MONDAY The Sun is lining up with Pluto, so you
must take care that you don't do tremendous damage to
your bank account. Usually you're a shrewd and canny
person, but there are times when you suddenly break
out and behave in the opposite way. Because you
generally have extremely good taste, this can be pricey.

15 TUESDAY Today Mercury is lining up with Pluto. This
may lead to minor adjustments in your social arrangements, so it might be a good idea to get on the telephone
and double-check with whoever it is you're supposed to
be spending time with. At work, concentration breaks

down, so it might be a good idea to deal with jobs that you can do with one hand tied behind your back.

16 WEDNESDAY Only by coming up with something inspired and original will you capture the attention of those who have an influence on your long-term future. Of course, your creativity may take a little time to flow, and you might be tempted to be pushy or sycophantic. Don't, because you will forfeit a lot more than you gain.

17 THURSDAY You seem to think that outward appearances count for a great deal in a world you've chosen to inhabit. For that reason you have taken steps to ensure that you will never be accused of letting the side down or trailing behind. The stars remind you that your inner being counts for far more than you may have realized recently. If, as is likely, you find yourself on the road to success, it's because of who you are and not what you appear to be.

18 FRIDAY This seems to be a hard-working day: hopefully you're finishing off any jobs that have been hanging around. A period of contemplation begins soon, giving you time to rethink ideas. Hesitation lingers in the stars, calling for patience all round. It's a time for saving money, rather than spending it. The best things in life are free.

19 SATURDAY A confident, hard-working phase will soon begin, but the stars taunt you with issues from the past. It's important that you try to see this from a different viewpoint now. Take a look at your need to control: it may not be doing you any favours. Once you begin to understand the problems buried deep in your subconscious, you'll make more progress with the outward aspects of life.

20 SUNDAY There's laughter in the air around you at work today, with everyone keen to help each other. This makes a welcome change after your recent uncertainty regarding your career, and it inspires a more sociable mood. The planets suggest a period of hard work ahead, but with your colleagues by your side, you'll easily get it done, with plenty of time left over for a rather more light-hearted undertaking.

21 MONDAY The Sun is about to move into the airy sign of Gemini. That's the rather secretive area of your chart, so this could mean that you'll prefer to work alone and quietly in the background, rather than sounding the trumpets and stepping into the limelight. Your instincts will be firing on all cylinders too, so it is important that you listen to them and don't tell yourself you're being silly.

22 TUESDAY Today the stars suggest that you are at your imaginative best. Use this in as positive a way as possible, and you will get the most out of the day and set up potential opportunities for the future. This might be a good time to plan a lively evening, so invite some friends around or go out on the town.

23 WEDNESDAY Today is the day of the new Moon, and
it occurs in the airy sign of Gemini. Your instincts are
really at their most impressive at this time, so do listen to
them. Remember that in the past you have seen the red
light and ignored it, only to regret it later.

24 THURSDAY Today Mercury is lining up with Uranus,
so there's bound to be a lively feel about this particular
day. Anything which happens unexpectedly should not
be viewed with suspicion, but thought about over a
period of time. Once you have done this you will realize
that you have a chance to shine, or perhaps to help
somebody else.

25 FRIDAY Although your financial prospects look more
promising than they have done for a while, there's still
work to be done. Start by putting your affairs in order,
then plan ahead. Unfortunately, associates may not give
you their support: in fact, they may be downright
evasive. However, the stars bring a fresh outlook in the
days to come, and you'll be content to push ahead on
your own then.

26 SATURDAY Your workload may feel heavier than
usual, so discriminate. Deal with immediate issues as
they arise, setting aside long-term projects for now. The
planets find you taking a look at your future. You'll
begin to see your ambitions in a different light: what
seemed impossible before now makes perfect sense.

27 SUNDAY The stars put you in a rather serious mood. This is hardly your normal form and causes concern from those around you. But it will be short-lived, and your mood becomes more playful as the planets move on. You're filled with inspiration during this time. Store it away for another time, though: your mind may be willing, but your heart is set on another venture right now.

28 MONDAY Today Mercury is lining up with Mars, so there'll be many minor changes where professional matters are concerned, and perhaps paperwork or some document that you're considering signing. Think long and hard, and wait until next month if that is at all possible.

29 TUESDAY You know how to grasp the nettle, but there's a possibility you might get stung just now. The planets suggest that you should take nothing for granted and tread carefully where other people's feelings are concerned, as wires are easily crossed. A nostalgic mood smoothes the waves during the days to come; relax with your family and friends, but don't ask too many questions.

30 WEDNESDAY Today the Sun is lining up with Neptune; consequently, you may be tempted into spending money or doing something creative or sociable. Romance is well starred too: just as long as you keep one foot on the ground, you won't get your generous heart crushed.

31 THURSDAY On the surface you still feel slightly
hyperactive, but deep down there is a growing sense
of satisfaction, because you know that a significant
hurdle is about to be crossed. You have been struggling
hard recently in order to find a more secure
base. Easier times are almost here, so you can afford to
be generous.

JUNE

THE SUN THIS MONTH will be drifting through the airy
sign of Gemini up until the 21st. This is a rather quiet area of
your chart: in many instances it represents your subconscious, which seems to be churning around quite a lot. The
tendency for you to rely on your instincts should continue if
you are to make the most out of life in all areas.

On the 22nd the Sun will be moving into your own sign,
filling you with solar power, confidence, and a get-up-and-go
that you have rarely experienced. It's a time for being less
unselfish and for putting your own needs before those of
other people; nobody is going to mind, because this phase
will only last for a few weeks.

Mercury continues in Gemini for the entire month, but
unfortunately goes into retrograde movement between the
4th and the 27th. On no account should you sign any
document or take important trips during this period: to do
so will be to invite complication and disappointment.

Venus remains in Aries during the first week, which is
the zenith of your chart, so you will continue to mix
business with pleasure, and it's a great time for forming
professional partnerships. If you want to approach a

member of the opposite sex at your workplace, act during this first week because the opportunity will pass once this period is over.

On the 7th Venus will be moving into Taurus, throwing a happy glow over your friends and acquaintances. Invitations are likely to pour in from all sides, and if you happen to be unattached then it's likely that someone will want to make an introduction. Pluck up your courage and accept: after all, you've got nothing to lose.

Mars continues on its weary way through the fiery sign of Sagittarius; therefore, those people you are financially dependent upon continue to be rather stressed and strained. If they carry on like this, they may very well make themselves ill, so it's up to somebody, namely you, to talk some common sense into them. Do make sure that they let off steam from time to time, if only for the sake of their health.

During June many of the planets are beneath the horizon on your birth chart, which seems to suggest that you'll be more intent on sorting out your personal life – whether it be the family, children or romance – rather than pushing yourself up the ladder of success. It looks as if you have your priorities right at this time.

Now look at the following *Daily Guides* for further information.

1   **FRIDAY** There's a lot of chat today, but not much action. Nothing is achieved without effort; if you don't do your bit, someone else may end up doing it for you, which you may regret. Look out for interesting developments in relationships very soon, but be wary of an introduction that could lead to something more intense than you had anticipated.

2 SATURDAY Your busy mind needs to find more concentrated focus today, as you may need to make a serious decision that could involve cutting your losses in one area of life. Spend part of the day with loved ones and enjoy sentimental moods. The planets will be taking a hard look at partnerships, both professional and personal. This is not a time to go it alone: use their strength to your advantage, and give your energy in return.

3 SUNDAY Take good care of your physical wellbeing today. You know your limitations: if you wear yourself out, you won't have the patience to deal with more testing days ahead. A question concerning property may need an answer in the week to come, and you'll need your wits about you, as you could be taken by surprise.

4 MONDAY Unfortunately, Mercury goes into retrograde movement, and as long as this continues you'd be most unwise to agree to go on important journeys or put your name to important documents. Mistakes are easily made under these conditions, but they're not so easily unmade: this is something you've probably experienced in the past and don't want to experience again.

5 TUESDAY Today the Sun is in a difficult aspect with Pluto, so you may get the feeling that your progress is being blocked, possibly unnecessarily. Luckily this is only a 24-hour annoyance and it will pass off tomorrow, so you can relax very soon.

6 WEDNESDAY Today is the day of the full Moon, and it occurs in the fiery sign of Sagittarius, the area of your chart devoted to your relationships with your workmates, and to health and routine. Should you feel a little under the weather, which you may very well do, then it might be a good idea to rest up this evening, no matter how tempting the social arrangements are. You can soon pick up on them in a couple of days time, when you'll be in tip-top shape.

7 THURSDAY Today Venus will be moving into the earthy sign of Taurus, encouraging sociability, peace and calm where friends are concerned. Therefore, if you need to ask for a favour or backing, or simply some support over something, this is the time to ask. Female friends are likely to be far more important than male, regardless of your own sex.

8 FRIDAY Don't put off until tomorrow what can be done today, because the planets show confusing arrangements and create misunderstandings all round you. That doesn't mean to say that your mind won't be filled with brilliant thoughts, though. Simply allow yourself time for reflection and meditation, and wait for a more appropriate time to publicize your ideas.

9 SATURDAY Today Mars is lining up with Uranus, so there's sure to be a lively feel about the day. Where work matters are concerned, things may happen completely out of the blue, but luckily you seem to be on your mettle and are able to cope with them rather than going into a flap. Better double-check your social arrangements too, as it's likely that they could change several times.

10 SUNDAY You will be very casual in your approach to other people today. Certainly you will be drawn to friendships, but without the need for personal ties. Unconventional activities could also stir your imagination, and because of this you are likely to be taking on a new activity or hobby. You will be more than happy to give advice to close contacts where it is needed.

11 MONDAY An awkward aspect in the stars dampens your enthusiasm. That isn't necessarily a bad thing though, as it allows time for your ideas to take shape and lets them hatch of their own accord. Meanwhile, concentrate your efforts on increasing intimacy with loved ones. The more you give, the more you'll get back, despite a slight hiccup.

12 TUESDAY The day ahead will be slow going where work is concerned, but you will find that you are looking for thorough determination. You alternate between intense activity and times where you need to retreat into the quiet, and that is perfectly healthy.

13 WEDNESDAY Today Venus is in a difficult aspect with Saturn, so there could be a disappointment where your social life is concerned, and it might be a good idea to ring first in order to find out what the state of play is. Romance may be a little bit difficult too, and others may fail to keep a promise that you believed they would. Try to be adaptable.

14 THURSDAY After the disappointment of yesterday, today seems to be a brighter day due to the fact that the

Sun is lining up with Jupiter. You're going to have a happy knack of being in the right place at the right time where your money, social life and love life are concerned. You're feeling optimistic and so is everyone around, so it's a good day.

15 FRIDAY Venus is in a difficult aspect with Neptune; therefore, you cannot believe everything you see or hear at this particular time. Instead, try to see through the fog to what is intended, because I think you'll find that your intuition will serve you well.

16 SATURDAY An inspired idea will make you sit up and think. There's no doubt that you have a vivid imagination and can be misled by it on occasions, but you may be right on the mark this time. Try a little double-checking by sounding out close companions whose judgement you trust.

17 SUNDAY Today the Sun is in a beautiful aspect with Mercury, so it looks as if you can gain on a financial level, either by taking a trip, meeting new people, or perhaps even signing a document. Certainly, by the time evening arrives, you should be in a mood for letting go and really enjoying yourself, and you will deserve it.

18 MONDAY Today Mercury lines up with Uranus, and you may be tempted to change your mind about a promise you have made to somebody else. In a word, don't, because you'll be storing up trouble and ruining your reputation for consistency and caring.

19 TUESDAY The stars bring a little light relief, because you find you are the centre of attention again. There will still be a need for discreet conversations, but you can begin to feel that your horizons are opening up all round. Start rehearsing what you want to say to get best results.

20 WEDNESDAY It may be that the committee style approach tests your patience, because you basically like keeping a grip yourself. Yet if you can open up to alternative viewpoints, especially from younger companions, you will make much faster headway. An intriguing phone call will make you smile.

21 THURSDAY Today is the day of the new Moon, and it occurs in the airy sign of Gemini. That is the area of your chart devoted to secrecy, your emotions and your instincts, and the latter certainly will be serving you well during this particular day, because you will be meeting many new people and will be working out exactly who you want to spend time with in future and who you don't. New Moons are always great times for making fresh starts.

22 FRIDAY Today the Sun will be moving into your sign, so you begin your solar year: this simply means that the Sun has returned to the place in the skies where it was on your birthday. Use this time for making a fresh start: it may be that you want to spruce up your image or change it altogether, or perhaps you want to let go of a relationship which is undermining your confidence. The latter seems more likely.

23 SATURDAY This may be a time when it will be necessary for you to accept changing conditions within the family. It may be that you are expected to accept added responsibility and make commitments. There are no instant solutions to this, and you should not allow yourself to be cajoled, pushed or pressured in any way. It may be necessary for you to do a bit of homework or research before you can decide what needs to be done in this direction.

24 SUNDAY You have no intention of letting the grass grow under your feet. These are rather heady days, when you are fully stretched and enjoying almost every moment of your activities at work or out in the community. One snap decision may work out better than you could possibly have expected.

25 MONDAY You're mentally alert and keen to spread your views to as wide an audience as possible. Just remember to keep your feet on the floor, since there is a danger you may forget to do reality checks along the way. Success is only ten per cent inspiration. The rest is sheer slog.

26 TUESDAY You can persuade partners to come clean by offering to keep their secrets safe; then you will have a much better chance of resolving whatever remaining muddles are holding you up. You're beginning to feel really restless, wanting more entertaining times and a freer lifestyle.

27 WEDNESDAY If you want to blow your own trumpet, then you must remember that you are kind, supportive and adaptable, but sometimes rather vague when it comes to firm commitments. Perhaps you're going to have to dig deeper for the answers you need today, and that will take time and persistence, but luckily you have both.

28 THURSDAY Today Mercury resumes direct movement, so you need not fear putting your signature to any important documents. This is also a good time for making travel arrangements, as the summer holidays are just over the horizon. If you act quickly, you might just be able to find a bargain, and you love to do that.

29 FRIDAY Looking in detail at all those loose ends around, you are now convinced you have everything taped. It has been a long slog, but you have every reason to feel satisfied that you have worked well without a great deal of support. Pat yourself on the back, and recognize your own achievements.

30 SATURDAY For all your tough exterior, you are a softy inside and particularly sentimental about family, so let yourself be seen with your heart on your sleeve for once. If you do not feel inclined to play the romantic, play the entertainer instead. You want to let your tensions out and relax: it'll do you a power of good.

JULY

THE SUN THIS MONTH will be swimming through the watery sign of Cancer until the 23rd. This of course is your sign, so you can make others see things from your point of view, providing you approach them in the right way. Be a little more forceful at work, but change tactics completely when dealing with friends or family, because if you try to twist anybody's arm I'm afraid you'll be slipping in the popularity polls, and you won't get your own way.

From the 24th till the end of the month, the Sun will be in the fiery sign of Leo, which is the area of your chart devoted to cash and possessions. According to the astrological aspects, some days you may be prepared to go out and do serious damage to your bank account with the credit cards, whilst on others you will shop around until you find something that is worth the price tag. You'll be improving not only your surroundings, but also yourself: maybe you're trying to take on a new image. As this is your time of the year, you can please yourself in the full knowledge that whatever you do is going to be well received. This latter part of the month is particularly good for those of you who work in the money professions. You always do have a canny eye for the material side of life, and this is exaggerated this month, so you could be picking up useful items, perhaps for the home or maybe for yourself, far more cheaply than usual. All in all, then, you could finish July a good deal better off than you started it.

Now look at the *Daily Guides* for further information.

1   SUNDAY The Sun today is lining up with Neptune, so there could be a certain amount of confusion where possessions or money matters are concerned. Little items could suddenly grow legs and go walkabout; you could waste a great deal of your time looking for them and getting more and more cross and frustrated. Therefore, it might be a good idea to get especially well organized on this day in order to avoid unnecessary stress. Double-check your social or romantic arrangements this evening too: you really can't take anything for granted.

2   MONDAY The astrological pattern today can mean one of two things: either you are sitting quietly letting old memories from the past come back, or you are talking to loved ones and coming to a sensible understanding of what you want for yourself. You don't feel inclined to rush around just yet, that's for sure. You're not quite ready to leap into action, for reasons that perhaps only you understand.

3   TUESDAY These few days of restlessness are almost at an end, so you are trying to collect your wits to see how you want to change your approach in the days ahead. There are constant gear shifts through the next few days, or even weeks: some are shifts up to a higher level, while others are downward shifts. Make all outstanding phone calls and visits that may be playing on your conscience, because then you'll feel more relaxed and able to get yourself together.

4   WEDNESDAY Today your money planet, the Sun, is lining up with Pluto, and if you're not careful you may finish up this day seriously out of pocket. It wouldn't be a good idea to spend too much time with your luxury-loving friends or contacts: their attitude to life could very easily rub off on you, and then you'll be berating yourself for being so weak-minded. It's a reasonably good time for making changes, just as long as they're not connected with your personal life.

5   THURSDAY Today is the day of the full Moon, and it occurs in your opposite sign of Capricorn. Unfortunately, this could mean a falling out with somebody else; if you allow that tenacious side of your character to take over, others may not be seeing you in the best light. As a Cancerian you invariably like to have your own way, but that is not the way to go on this particular day, unless you want a relationship to come to an end. Furthermore, do not take your responses to situations and other people too seriously, because the full Moon has a way of exaggerating everything.

6   FRIDAY Today Venus will be moving into the airy sign of Gemini, and that's the rather secretive area of your chart. Consequently, there's an inclination for you to perhaps not be as straightforward as you might be where emotional matters are concerned. Do bear in mind that if you try to deceive another person you will most assuredly be found out. Put yourself in their shoes, and you may realize how this could feel: then you may be able to avoid it.

7 SATURDAY Make sure that you have all the financial paperwork in good order. You'll find you don't have the time or the inclination during the days and weeks ahead to do much other than rush along helter-skelter, so this is your last chance to put certain pieces of the financial jigsaw in the correct place. Don't waste it.

8 SUNDAY Your day ahead will be well organized at work; it's a good day for cash, but also for extravagance. Mind you, you can probably afford to be a little bit silly, just as long as you don't go to extremes. You're still not clear where you are heading, but you are enjoying the trip, and that's important. However, you must find time to reflect quietly on the past.

9 MONDAY Today the Sun is lining up with Mars, and because of this a mood of impetuosity could strike so that you may run amok and ruin your balance books. Best to stay away from friends who are either better off than yourself, or who are of an extravagant and wasteful nature. If you fail to do so, I'm afraid you could live to regret this 24-hour period.

10 TUESDAY You know you need to find a straight-forward way of communicating, which may mean using a mixture of charm and persistence. Do not become discouraged if your comments are not taken on board first time, but keep trying with as much diplomacy as you can muster up. When you decide to do this, you can be unbeatable.

11 WEDNESDAY How to be extravagant whilst saving money at the same time is puzzling even your fertile imagination, but you do have contradictory influences at the moment around your finances. If you are discussing cash, try to be cool and gracious. You will notice the brakes will come off quite suddenly if you do this.

12 THURSDAY Today Mercury is lining up with Jupiter, so your imagination is at its most fertile; therefore, this is an excellent day for those of you who work in artistic or creative occupations. Short trips and interviews should be successful too: you'll make a good impression, and life should run smoothly in these directions. Play your astrological cards right during the day, and you will have reason to celebrate this evening.

13 FRIDAY Today Mercury will be moving into your sign, and this will most definitely liven up your entire personality. Your brainpower will speed up quite a good deal, and other people will be impressed by your efficiency too. You have a good couple of weeks for any kind of travelling, legal matters, or for making minor changes, so use this time well.

14 SATURDAY Venus continues in the airy sign of Gemini, which is a good omen, because it'll bring out all the best sides to your character, making you more loving, courteous and generous. Furthermore, there's a strong chance that you could meet someone very important during the next few weeks. If you already have a partner, though, you will need to exercise some self-control, otherwise you will be storing up a good deal of problems and bad feelings around you.

15 SUNDAY Jupiter has now moved into your sign, so you begin a couple of months or so where Lady Luck is definitely on your side. Opportunity knocks, so be ready to snap it up. The only negative side to this astrological placing is the possibility that you could put on weight, but then again you wouldn't be a Cancerian if you didn't have this tendency, because you do have a sweet tooth and a love of good food. However, if you want to retain your sylph-like figure, a certain amount of willpower will be required. This is certainly not a good time for trying to diet, anyway.

16 MONDAY You seem to be rushing around trying to act as some kind of mediator, but quite frankly you feel distance from companions. The astrological line-up today sees the start of a period when you may be standing on the sidelines, which you may not enjoy. Nevertheless, do not be too eager to rush forward to volunteer for extra chores: you are likely to take on more than you can comfortably chew.

17 TUESDAY Today Venus will be lining up with Pluto in a not very satisfactory fashion. There's a suggestion here that home, property and matters related to your love life could be stalling badly. You may feel that you want to move on and to change your life, but perhaps this is not the best day for doing so.

18 WEDNESDAY You know you need more time to consider your long-term choices and options, but there has been precious little space recently for reflection. Only you are in a position to know what has become more of a burden than it is worth recently. Once in a while everyone needs to clear the excess baggage out of their lives, and this seems to be one of those times for you.

19 THURSDAY Fortunately Mars decides to resume direct movement today, so any frustration you may have felt in connection with work and other professional matters will slowly begin to fade away, and progress will pick up, if only slowly. Male colleagues could be a bit tetchy, so you'd better be as respectful as you possibly can, without crawling, of course.

20 FRIDAY Today is the day of the new Moon, and it's an important one because it falls in your sign. You have a couple of days, then, for making some major changes, perhaps to your appearance or to your situation. Anything you want out of life, within reason, can be yours, providing you push ahead in a determined fashion. So see what you can do. Anyone new you meet today is likely to be very important.

21 SATURDAY One older friend is being cool to the point of sounding critical – which, being a sensitive water sign, you dislike – but if you can take their advice on board you may come to realize that they are just being practical. Your career is about to take off soon, so you need to be clearly focussed.

22 SUNDAY The stars are contradictory today, but you can still do your duties whilst indulging yourself at the same time. Just keep impressing all the influential people in your circle. The stars will very soon be releasing you from pressure, and then you'll be very glad that you remained patient.

23 MONDAY The Sun is now poised to move into the fiery sign of Leo; that, of course, is the financial area of your chart and a placing well worth welcoming. It's likely that you have spent a good deal of money recently, and this placing of the Sun will tend to make you more frugal and sensible, so that you should be provided with a chance to save a little bit of cash. Furthermore, those of you who work in the money professions are assured a lucrative and enjoyable time on the professional front.

24 TUESDAY You are likely to feel you have far too much on your plate, and this is making you irritable at times. Try to raise your sights slightly and only pursue what is important. You're sifting and sorting out your options on all sorts of subjects, and for that you need to mix in more stimulating company.

25 WEDNESDAY If you feel that you have been treated less than generously or cut off from support which was once there, you need to be more straightforward about asking for what you need. The astrological setup today is not a disaster, but a lesson about cooperation, so bear that in mind. Maybe you will have to give in different ways in order to get help.

26 THURSDAY Being of a passionate nature, you never like superficial or detached relationships. Even less do you like letting go, but life is all about swings and roundabouts. Sometimes you move in, and sometimes you have to move out. The planets today will push you back to work for a few weeks, so get into good shape if possible.

27 FRIDAY Today Venus is in a difficult aspect with Uranus, and because of this friends and contacts will be less cooperative than usual. Because there's a certain amount of frustration around, you may be feeling the strain; therefore, my advice to you is to either get in an early night or at least relax at home this evening. Hectic social whirls will really not appeal, and you could alienate other people if you take part in them.

28 SATURDAY You are probably getting a bit tired of hearing about work and health, but they have been important factors for you recently and will continue to be so with the current planetary setup. Luckily, there will be more than enough pleasant distractions in the days ahead to keep you happily occupied, so you needn't fret.

29 SUNDAY Socially and romantically you have not had enough to keep you sparkling recently. Although you have a reputation for being a workaholic, you are nevertheless a sensual sign. Maybe you are not ready for a rave-up, but try to find some time for fun; then

you'll be able to settle quietly at home for a few weeks.
Enjoy it.

30 MONDAY Today Saturn is lining up with Neptune,
and because of this you really can't believe everything
other people tell you. It's not that they're being deliberately deceptive, but they are disorganized and unsure, so
rely on your own gut feelings instead: that way, nothing
untoward should happen. Romantically, today could be
interesting but not at all serious.

31 TUESDAY Today Mercury will be moving into the
fiery sign of Leo and that's the area of your chart
devoted to your earning power, spending, and all
matters related to cash. Mercury seems to be hinting
that you'll be either travelling for the sake of money or
perhaps signing an important document over the next
few weeks. Keep your eyes peeled for opportunities,
because they are there for the taking.

AUGUST

THE SUN THIS MONTH continues to coast through the
fiery sign of Leo up until the 23rd. This, of course, is the
financial area of your chart, and while this astrological
placing exists you will be reluctant to spend your money.
This is no bad thing, because it's likely that early in the year
you made a great hole in your accounts. Furthermore, this is
a particularly lucky time for dealing with people in the
money professions: any meetings that take place are sure to
be successful. Therefore, if you want to extend your bank

overdraft, which you rarely do, or perhaps get financial advice, you have an ideal time for such actions.

On the 24th the Sun will move along into the earthy sign of Virgo. Once this occurs it may be difficult for you to sit still for too long: you'll be rushing hither and thither, and if the chance to mix business with travel crops up then you should snatch it, as it'll be very lucky for you. Those of you professionally involved in sales – and also, perhaps, advertising – are in for a fruitful and lucky time. However, on a more personal level, you may find your time being taken up by a brother or a sister who seems to have got into something of a mess. Luckily, with your shrewd good sense you'll soon be able to sort them out, so there's really not a great deal to worry about.

Mercury will be in Leo up until the 14th. Consequently, travelling or contracts that are connected with cash will be extremely lucky for you, and you mustn't hesitate to put your signature to them, always assuming that you have read them through thoroughly.

After the 15th, Mercury joins the Sun in Virgo. This will certainly ginger up your grey matter and make decision-making much quicker and more efficient than usual. Any chance to travel for the sake of pleasure, your personal life, or business should be snapped up, though it might be a good idea to double-check your car, just in case it decides to let you down. Mind you, this is unlikely to happen unless you choose a very bad day for setting off.

Venus enters your sign on the 2nd, and so for the entire month your charm will be apparent to everybody. Physically you're positively blooming, and you'll be attracting the opposite sex to you in droves. This is a lovely position to find yourself in, so do make sure that you make the most of it. If you are already in a long-standing relationship, you may be thinking about taking the next step towards becoming engaged or married; if you have decided to take this momentous decision, then you have picked an ideal time.

Unfortunately, Mars continues its rather laborious way through the fiery sign of Sagittarius. Because of this, you still need to take a good deal of care of yourself, because minor accidents caused by hot and sharp objects are a threat. Furthermore, if there are any bugs hanging around, you're going to be picking them up; therefore, if somebody close has a bout of the sneezes, then it might be a good idea to keep them at a distance until they are better. Other people might think you're being something of a hypochondriac, but it is better to stay hale and hearty if you possibly can.

The pattern the stars make this month seems to suggest that you'll be more concerned with putting the finishing touches to situations, financial affairs, work and so on, rather than starting anything new, and if that's the way you feel then you should go with your instincts.

Now look at the *Daily Guides* for further information.

1 WEDNESDAY Domestic business seems to be a high priority at the moment, and so does sorting out emotional tensions, perhaps within the family. You seem to have found just the right approach. Once you have cleared this out of the way, you will find that you are definitely on your toes, chatting animatedly and racing around in circles. Boredom won't even get a look-in, thank goodness.

2 THURSDAY Today Venus will be moving into your sign, and that's good news because it will be livening

up your social life. Romantic possibilities will cross
your path, and you'll be looking good, feeling good,
and playing the opportunist. You could well meet
someone very important during this period, and if you
already have someone special in your life, you couldn't
have a better time for considering engagement or
marriage. Those of you in the luxury trades or the arts
will be putting out a good deal of work which will
impress other people.

3   FRIDAY Anyone who thinks you'll be defeated by
limitations imposed on your time, money or freedom
had better think again. You never were a coward or a
quitter, but at the moment you seem more determined
than ever to be the one who calls the shots. Failure is a
word that simply isn't in your vocabulary at the
moment.

4   SATURDAY Today is the day of the full Moon, and it
occurs in the airy sign of Aquarius. This is a part of your
chart devoted to those you are financially dependent
upon, so you could very well find that your boss or your
mate is suffering a certain amount of irritation, which,
of course, they may very well take out on you. Because
of this, you must be as understanding and supportive as
you possibly can. Also, remember that full Moons are
always a good time for putting the finishing touches to
things.

5   SUNDAY Today your money planet, the Sun, is lining
up beautifully with Pluto. As a result, there's likely to be
a theme of change about the day, especially in

connection with your social life, but also where cash matters are concerned. There'll be many chances for you to enjoy yourself this evening, and you can afford to be choosy: just make sure that you can afford whatever you decide to do, or you will regret it.

6 MONDAY Today the Sun is in a difficult aspect with Saturn. Maybe you didn't take yesterday's advice, in which case you will be feeling a little bit depressed by your depleted bank account. Furthermore, someone close is being rather bumptious and domineering; although you may sense that this is not the time to put them in their place, you must do so as soon as the right mood and atmosphere descends.

7 TUESDAY Refuse to let anyone pull rank or undermine your authority as a means of clipping your wings when you're doing so well. You do, perhaps without knowing it, sometimes stick your neck out by broadcasting your latest triumphs and acquisitions. A slightly lower profile might help matters quite a lot.

8 WEDNESDAY Today Venus is in a beautiful aspect with Neptune, so there's a rather nostalgic and romantic feel about this particular day. Furthermore, if you work in anything creative, you'll be doing exceptionally well. However, there may be an inclination for you to become totally carried away, and it might be a good idea to make sure that you double-check everything. If you happen to be fancy-free, get out this evening, because romance seems to be on the cards.

9   **THURSDAY** It will be a pity if certain formalities are allowed to impinge on a partnership or a romantic affair. The planets right now are highlighting the many possibilities that are open to you, but Saturn is reminding you that there's unfinished business to attend to first. Instinct will help you to find a solution in record time.

10 **FRIDAY** A tendency to cling to what a certain relationship can provide will fade as quickly as it appeared. Meanwhile, remember that there are some people who cannot bear to be leaned upon, and you must take care not to spoil a good thing. Make yourself scarce until you feel strong again, which you will do very soon.

11 **SATURDAY** Today Mercury is lining up with Uranus in a rather unsatisfactory way, which means that any kind of travelling is going to be fraught with frustration. You may find that you and other people are mentally changeable, and the whole day could go to waste unless you slow down and think things through a little bit more calmly than usual.

12 **SUNDAY** Today Venus is lining up with Pluto, which suggests that your social life is picking up quite considerably: you may even be spoiled for choice. Be selective, and make sure that you get the maximum out of your time, so that you'll have nothing to regret.

13 **MONDAY** Try not to let financial concerns turn into emotional insecurities. The planets today may overemphasize a slight problem, which you would happily shrug off at any other time. So much of your life is built on firm foundations that it's a pity to destroy it over a fairly everyday bill or debt.

14 TUESDAY The fact that your strategies are often quite conventional means that others would never expect you to use emotional blackmail to get what you want. However, you may be finding it difficult to suppress your feelings over work or money matters. Remember, shock tactics sometimes do more harm than good.

15 WEDNESDAY Today Mercury will be moving into the sign of Virgo, and that's the area of your chart which rules the mind and short-distance travelling. Your intellect is going to be in great shape, and you'll have lots of good ideas, so keep a pen handy. Those of you who are travelling from place to place should find it relatively easy to do so, with the result that you'll have plenty of energy left over this evening for getting out and enjoying yourself.

16 THURSDAY Today the Sun is in a difficult aspect with Uranus, and because of this there may be a financial loss or complication, or perhaps you will mislay something of sentimental value. Double-check your possessions when leaving home; perhaps the best advice would be not to take anything of particular value with you.

17 FRIDAY Today Jupiter is lining up with Neptune, so this could be a rather muddle-headed day. You may spend a good deal of your time looking for things that have gone astray, or perhaps there will be a misunderstanding between yourself and other people. However, with a little bit of determination, you should be able to get through once you have thought things out sensibly.

18 SATURDAY With so many jobs and duties outstanding, you might do well to enlist the help of someone to whom you feel a strong attachment. Not only would this get a number of jobs out of the way, but it could reveal an aspect of a relationship that you hadn't considered up till now. You're better off than you think.

19 SUNDAY Today is the day of the new Moon, and luckily for you it falls in the cash area of your chart. This means that money that is owed will roll in, and there may even be opportunities for you to glean bargains or perhaps swell your bank account. Be alert to every chance on the materialistic level, and you'll have little to chastise yourself for. A good time, too, for new beginnings in all areas.

20 MONDAY Don't make a martyr of yourself over someone who is not nearly as helpful as they might appear. The combination of the planets today renders it difficult for you to see things in their true perspective, but deep down you must know that a certain amount of tough love wouldn't be out of place. Don't weaken.

21 TUESDAY Today Venus is in a friendly aspect with Uranus, so you could be making new friends and contacts, possibly with unusual people and quite suddenly. Such a day is likely to give you plenty of food for thought, but don't confuse a friendship with a

possible romance; this is, I'm afraid, a common
Cancerian pitfall.

22 WEDNESDAY Even though you know some people
haven't dealt with you openly and honestly, you must
think carefully before taking the matter to someone
with power or influence. The last thing you want is a
scene which could lead to a state of open warfare.
Wait a day or two before deciding exactly what you
should do.

23 THURSDAY Today is likely to be a lively one, thanks
to the aspect between Mars and Uranus. People who
pop up suddenly into your life could be of the utmost
importance, so take note and try to find out what's
going on beneath the surface. This evening is an ideal
time for your personal life, though any romance is
likely to be based on sex rather than on anything else,
so don't kid yourself.

24 FRIDAY Today the Sun will be moving into the
earthy sign of Virgo, the part of your chart devoted to
the mind and to short-distance travelling. Any chance
to pay visits, be they professional or personal, should
be snapped up, because failure to do so could lead to
disappointment at a later date. Those of you who have
had trouble with your bicycle, motorcycle or car should
easily find someone to put this right for you, so there's
no need to go into a panic. This evening is a light-
hearted time, so don't start reading something that
doesn't exist into the actions of other people.

25 SATURDAY Pluto has now resumed direct movement, and this is good news, because it is likely that matters related to children, creativity and even casual romance have been somewhat complicated recently. That is now likely to be a thing of the past, and you can finally loosen your stays and relax.

26 SUNDAY All the time you're wondering whether you're doing the right thing, you are in danger of doing the wrong one. No-one else doubts your skills or acumen, and you must not allow your insecurities to work against you. Focus on all that is positive about your work or reputation. There's plenty of it.

27 MONDAY Several exciting possibilities are opening up before you, but you must be prepared to make decisions – some of them irrevocable – along the way. The planets' influence will do a lot to remind you of the fact that you, and you alone, are responsible for the way in which you use your unique gifts and resources. You must have always known there would come a time when you'd have to prove your worth, and this is it. Don't worry: you should do well.

28 TUESDAY Today Venus will be moving into Leo, which is the financial area of your chart. Because of this, you'll be gaining through cooperation with other people, through anything artistic or creative, and also, perhaps, from sheer luck, although that doesn't give you permission to go out and act like a crazy person. If you've any Leos in your circle, then they're going to be extremely friendly, affectionate and willing to help you out, but you must make sure that you don't take advantage of them.

29 WEDNESDAY It's not very often that you can fritter away time or money purely for your own enjoyment, so you must use an unusual situation to your advantage. After all, you have needs and desires like everybody else, and if you continue to ignore them you may start to show signs of resentment. Have a wonderful time.

30 THURSDAY You might think you will never unravel a mix-up over who should pay for what. However, the situation isn't as complicated as you imagine. The secret is to keep any emotion out of the picture, as you don't want to start something you'll never be able to stop. Stick to the facts, and make sure everyone else does the same.

31 FRIDAY It is likely that you are feeling more confident and secure, and in the next few weeks you will be forming new relationships and ties which will support you and your ideas for some time to come. Regarding old alliances, it is likely that you will have to decide fairly soon whether you can cope with them and whether they are necessary; if not, it may be time to make a change.

SEPTEMBER

DURING SEPTEMBER, the Sun will continue to drift along in the earthy sign of Virgo up until the 23rd. Before this date your mind will be as clear as a bell, so it's an ideal time for making important decisions. Any chances to go on short trips, whether for social, romantic or professional reasons, should not be ignored, because you do so at your peril. Some of you may find that your method of transport – that is, your car, motorbike or bicycle – gives you some trouble; therefore, check thoroughly before leaving home, or you could find yourself well and truly stranded.

On the 24th the Sun will be drifting into the airy sign of Libra, and that's the area of your chart devoted to home, family and property, which are all matters that are dear to your heart. When it comes to socializing, you'll prefer to do so at home rather than being too adventurous. Guests will be in for a treat, because you invariably spoil them and spend too much money, but that's part of your character, because you're a cherishing person.

Mercury will be in Libra from the 2nd onwards, and because of this there may be some new faces for you to meet where work is concerned. There may also be important contracts and perhaps business trips. Unfortunately, this is also the area of your chart devoted to health, and Mercury seems to suggest you could be suffering from exhaustion from time to time. The best thing to do is to pace yourself, so that you can cope with everything as efficiently as you would like.

Venus remains in Leo, the cash area of your chart, until the 21st; therefore, there is a lucky glow over finances, especially if you are involved in the arts or if you're in any kind of professional partnership. Regardless of your own sex, women are going to be important when it comes to swelling your bank account, so at least give them a listen before you dismiss what they have to say.

On the 22nd Venus will be moving into Virgo. This throws a rosy glow over short-distance travelling and also your mind, which is going to be at its most creative;

consequently, if you have an artistic job, you'll certainly be doing extremely well. Furthermore, Venus will bring casual romance into your life, but don't blow it up into something more important until at least a month or so has passed, otherwise you'll finish up getting hurt.

Mars will at last be moving into your opposite sign of Capricorn on the 9th. This will be enhancing your relationships, but it is perhaps not the best time in the world for looking for romance. What we have here are strong sexual attractions: face them for what they are, enjoy them, take care and know when it is time to move on. Unfortunately, Mars so placed can make you accident prone, so you must be extremely careful where hot and sharp objects are concerned. Some of you may even suffer from a bout of food poisoning, so double-check the cleanliness of utensils if eating out in restaurants. Nobody is out to harm you, of course, but accidents do happen, probably through carelessness, and this is the time when this might just occur.

Because Saturn will be moving into retrograde action on the 27th, it's likely that partnerships could become unduly complicated until this state of affairs rectifies itself. Therefore, you'll need to tread carefully and be as thoughtful as you possibly can.

The pattern the stars make this month is a rather scattered one, which suggests that you'll find it easier to hop from project to project and person to person, rather than concentrating your energies in any serious way. Naturally, if your work requires any sort of detail, this could cause some problems, so it might be a good idea to be a bit more scrupulous: that will save you a great deal of trouble.

Now look at the *Daily Guides* for further information.

1 **SATURDAY** Today Venus is in a difficult aspect with Neptune, so you really can't believe all that you are told by members of your family. It's not that they're out to deceive you; it's more likely they are deceiving themselves. Property matters could also be a source of annoyance, so shelve them for a 24-hour period: that won't do any harm.

2 **SUNDAY** Today is the day of the full Moon, and it occurs in the watery sign of Pisces. Matters related to further education could be a little bit woolly and confused; therefore, if you are student you may need to double-check things. Mail that comes in from abroad may also be muddled, and you may have to make contact in order to sort out what on earth is going on. Mind you, full Moons are always a good time for putting the finishing touches to anything.

3 **MONDAY** Mercury has now moved into Libra, and this will be spicing up your home life. It looks as if you'll be having an above average number of visitors during the next few weeks. Naturally, as a Cancerian, you are a caring and generous host, so home entertaining could do you a great deal of good, perhaps with business contacts, or simply within the family.

4 **TUESDAY** Today the Sun is in a difficult aspect with Pluto, so where finances are concerned you could go completely over the top, perhaps in an effort to please somebody else. However, you mustn't do this to your own detriment or to that of your bank manager, otherwise you'll be hearing from him or her in a rather unpleasant way.

5　WEDNESDAY The knowledge or information you need to impress a group of individuals cannot be learnt or acquired. However, the stars today should ensure that your antennae are so finely tuned that answers will arrive as and when you need them, allowing you to get what you want.

6　THURSDAY Minor upsets between yourself and a loved one need not cause alarm. Provided you let the joint forces of the stars open up your mind to a new way of dealing with ongoing problems, you should have little to worry about. Don't be afraid to let go of what is redundant or out of date.

7　FRIDAY Don't overreact to the suggestion that partnership difficulties are the thin end of the wedge, but do try to bring a little magic into a situation which is showing signs of fatigue. Imagination is a wonderful thing, and rarely has yours been as fertile as it is now. Use it as only you know how.

8　SATURDAY You want to say something to loved ones, but you have no idea how they will take it. What you have overlooked is the possibility that your behaviour may already have given the game away. Don't wait so long that details become distorted through speculation. Whatever the news, it must discussed, and soon.

9 **SUNDAY** Today Mars moves into your opposite sign of Capricorn, which isn't altogether good news because it will make the other people in your life rather bad-tempered and impatient, and it's hard to imagine you getting through this month without some kind of altercation. On the other hand, there is a possibility that just for once you will not be out looking for the love of your life; you will be quite happy to satisfy your physical desires, and there's nothing wrong with this just as long as you take the necessary precautions.

10 **MONDAY** Today Mercury is lining up with Pluto. This may make you rather capricious when it comes to making any kind of decision, so where possible decisions should be shelved for at least 24 hours. If you push ahead now, you may have to retrace your steps, and this could lead to frustration.

11 **TUESDAY** Everyone knows how well you function within certain perimeters, but there is a possibility that those boundaries might soon be removed, and you'll have to rely on your own initiative a great deal more. Anyone who has ever doubted your ability to be self-motivated is about to be proved wrong.

12 **WEDNESDAY** Today Venus is in a friendly aspect with Pluto, and for some of you this could mean a wild attraction which you may mistake for love. For others, artistic work may be prone to interruption. There's no point in getting hot under the collar about this: perhaps it will give you the chance to double-check what you

have done or presented and realize perhaps that there
may be one or two holes that need mending.

13 THURSDAY There are times when you have to forgo
the chance to involve yourself in something new,
exciting or profitable and deal with long-standing obligations instead. But in the near future you'll come across
something that's too good to miss, and somehow you'll
find a way to pursue it. It will be worth the effort.

14 FRIDAY Today the Sun is lining up with Uranus, so
don't expect everything to run according to plan,
especially where financial matters are concerned.
Furthermore, you may spend a great deal of your time
looking for items which have been mislaid and seem to
be deliberately hiding from you. Naturally this is
irritating, but I'm afraid it happens to everyone
sometimes, and now it's your turn.

15 SATURDAY An invitation to revisit the past or to
rekindle an old friendship might not prove popular with
a loved one who feels slightly ill at ease. This episode
could provide the opportunity to establish a set of guide-
lines which will help you with a similar situation in the
future. Make it work for you.

16 SUNDAY It may seem that, however hard you work at
a particular relationship, there are areas which prove
difficult to resolve. But perhaps you have never put into
words what your heart and mind are really saying. Try
it. The impact it has could be what is needed to breathe
new life into something truly worthwhile.

17 MONDAY Today is the day of the new Moon, and it occurs in the earthy sign of Virgo. This is a great day for personal shopping, for expressing how you feel, and for being adventurous this evening when it comes to looking for fun or even romance. When it comes to making any kind of decision, your intuitions are razor sharp, so make sure that you listen to them.

18 TUESDAY Today Mercury is in a difficult aspect with Uranus, and because of this you may change your mind several times during this day, chopping and changing to the frustration of those around you. Take some time out to think things through carefully before you open your mouth, otherwise you could very well put your foot in it.

19 WEDNESDAY A chance encounter is likely to fire your imagination, and you'll be keen to learn more about a place, person or topic that you've always thought of as unusual or rarefied. There are those who can offer inspiration and enlightenment, but first you must prove that your need is genuine. Begin now.

20 THURSDAY Others seem to assume that your ambitious streak is driven by financial incentives, but deep down you know you couldn't do a good job for money alone. Of course, you can't be entirely impractical, but if you're prepared to relinquish one or two material advantages, you'll gain a lot more in other ways.

21 FRIDAY Having tried to follow the accepted route to a particular place, position or situation, you'll soon realize that you must adopt a less conventional stance if you are to get what you want. The combination of the planets today will encourage you to take the sort of risk which, if it pays off, will provide you with a short cut to wherever it is you want to be. Even if it doesn't do the trick the first time around, it very soon will, so keep trying.

22 SATURDAY Today Venus will be moving into the earthy sign of Virgo, adding a creative streak to your mind and imagination. It's also possible that you may meet potential admirers whilst going about your everyday business, so keep your eyes peeled just in case. It's a good time, too, for letting other people know exactly what you think and feel.

23 SUNDAY The Sun is about to move into Libra. This is the area of your chart devoted to home and property matters, which seem to be dominant at the moment. Some of you may be entertaining at home far more than usual. Others may be feeling restless in their current abode: if you are looking for a new home, you may well find one at the right price and in the right place.

24 MONDAY Although your ideas may be called fanciful, your individuality and inventiveness are secretly envied by many. Be proud that you're not one of the crowd, and treat any criticism as what it is: sour grapes. Nothing and no-one must be allowed to crush your creativity or to put you in an emotional straitjacket.

25 TUESDAY Resources may be limited and budgets tight, but that can't stop you from producing something which is guaranteed to surprise and delight you. The planets will provide all the inspiration you need, whilst the Sun makes sure that your efforts are seen and appreciated by all the right people at the right time, and that's always important.

26 WEDNESDAY Concentrate on ideas that catch your imagination, and trust your own abilities. You'll soon see that you have every reason to believe in yourself. The spotlight continues to shine on the creative and artistic area of your chart, with the added bonus of you being able to make money from your craft.

27 THURSDAY Today Saturn goes into retrograde movement, which means that your relationships may go through a complicated phase. Furthermore, if you wish to approach people in order to seek some kind of assistance from them, they may be rather elusive, and you're going to need a great deal of that Cancerian tenacity to get through to them.

28 FRIDAY You can really get things accomplished during this day. You will begin to feel more secure about yourself and less inclined to hide your talents. It's a time for you to embark on the process of learning and of gaining experience. Complications disappear, and, as you reach for the deeper dimensions of life, your close relationships grow all the more powerful.

29 SATURDAY Today there seems to be a rather explosive aspect between Mars and Pluto, and because of this you must not take anything for granted: if you do, you will be disappointed. Changes may be taking place at work, too, but just be flexible and you'll be able to cope confidently.

30 SUNDAY Today the Sun is lining up with Neptune, so if you work in anything creative you'll be putting plenty of effort into work and producing good results. This evening, double-check all your arrangements, particularly if they are romantic: somebody could have their wires crossed, and it might be you for a change.

OCTOBER

THIS MONTH THE SUN will be drifting along in the airy sign of Libra up until the 23rd, and that, of course, is the area of your chart devoted to the home, property and family. Such matters are likely to take precedence over everything else for a change, and your increased attention and caring approach will be generating the love and cooperation that is needed. Furthermore, it's a good time for asking friends around for a drink or a meal, particularly if you want to get to know them better.

From the 24th, the Sun will be sailing through the watery sign of Scorpio, and that's the area of your chart devoted to sports, children, social life and casual romance. It looks as if there is a great deal of fun in store for you, so throw yourself into the fray, and make sure that you get the most out of your life.

Mercury will be situated in Libra all month. As a result, there seems to be a great deal of activity going on at home: you'll be having plenty of visitors, and minor decisions will be made between yourself and those you live with. If you're looking for a new home, then this is an excellent time for finding one, and also for exchanging contracts.

Venus, too, will be situated in Libra for the second half of the month, urging you to beautify your surroundings and to keep your house busy with a stream of visitors. If you do decide to improve your surroundings, you couldn't have picked a better time: your excellent taste will be apparent to all of your friends and your family.

Mars will be drifting along in the earthy sign of Capricorn up until the 27th, and that, of course, is your opposite sign. Consequently, there will be a considerable amount of activity going on in your intimate relationships. However, it is important that you remember that your hormones are leaping around like crazy, and you must not mistake this for anything deeper; if you do, you could finish up getting hurt, and that would be a great pity. Once again you may be accident prone, so be careful when driving and when in the kitchen or the bathroom, as this is where most accidents occur.

Mars will be entering Aquarius on the 28th. Therefore, during the last few days of this month, those you are financially dependent upon may be stressed out and in something of a panic, so provide a soothing influence: they will be forever grateful.

The pattern the stars make this month suggests that you will begin many relationships, situations and perhaps jobs, but may be reluctant or unable to finish them for the time being. Try to draw up a list of priorities, then tackle whatever is most important and work your way down. In that way you will at least be functioning efficiently and constructively.

Now look at the *Daily Guides* for further information.

1   MONDAY Today Venus is in a beautiful aspect with Mars, so there is peace and harmony wherever you go. Furthermore, you have an excellent time for pestering estate agents or solicitors if you are trying to exchange contracts. It's a good time for sports and romance, although the latter has a predominantly sexual feel about it, so don't get carried away.

2   TUESDAY Today is the day of the full Moon, and it occurs in the fiery sign of Aries. It's possible then that you are hoping to hear from abroad, or perhaps in connection with further education. If so, you may be disappointed, but only for a 24-hour period, so there's no need to get too upset. As always with full Moons, it's a great time for putting the finishing touches to anything.

3   WEDNESDAY Mars today is lining up with Pluto, so there's certainly an energetic feel about this day. However, on a more personal level, your sexual appetite may be blocked for one reason or another; perhaps your partner has other things to think about and is feeling uncooperative or worried. The best thing you can do is be cherishing and caring, then this matter will soon resolve itself.

4   **THURSDAY** Today Mars is in aspect with Saturn, so there's a rather frustrating feel about this particular day. Relationships are prone to stress, strain and disagreement; somebody is going to have to keep a sense of perspective, and it might just as well be you. If you're out driving with a mate this evening, make sure that they take their time.

5   **FRIDAY** The overall perspective of your world is set to benefit from the stars. Some of you will take the learning track and set your sights on a topic that fills you with inspiration, while others will get the opportunity to travel much further afield. Whichever it happens to be, your view on life will change, and you will become much the wiser for today's aspects: they will add breadth and colour to your life in a delightfully indulgent fashion.

6   **SATURDAY** The stars today seem to be urging you towards security, but certain aspects still agitate your restless spirit. Avoid doing anything too impulsive, especially where property is concerned, and spend this evening with your family, as this will benefit you.

7   **SUNDAY** Today the Sun will be lining up with Pluto; therefore, it looks as if you're going to be spending money on your home or perhaps on entertaining this evening. You must make sure that you don't go completely overboard, otherwise you'll be in dire straits at a later date. Your home, of course, is your castle, but that doesn't mean it's got to look like one.

8   MONDAY In the very near future you'll see that you have every reason to believe in yourself. The spotlight continues to shine on the creative and artistic area of your chart, and you should benefit from this financially. This evening looks set fair for romance.

9   TUESDAY Today Venus is lining up with Uranus, so there could be one or two surprises sprung upon you by friends or acquaintances. Mind you, it looks as if there is more good than bad luck hanging around this day, so count your blessings and cope with any slight difficulties with aplomb and patience.

10 WEDNESDAY The planets are asking you to understand yourself better, to face your fears and to accept the less desirable aspects of your life. Then you'll be free to move ahead with more worldly matters and to do something intellectually satisfying. Close friends will listen to your ideas in the days ahead, and someone special will be hanging on your every word.

11 THURSDAY An opportunity is there to make your life much richer. Whether this is material or spiritual fortune rather depends on your values. Perhaps you should keep them to yourself for the time being. People are certainly willing to help you, but you are the one who has to make the decisions at the end of the day.

12 FRIDAY You won't need to stray very far from your everyday world to find the answers you're looking for. In fact, a close relative could provide the first clue. However, your curiosity may drive you further afield, but do check carefully as you go: there's a touch of disorganization among the stars which might affect your arrangements.

13 SATURDAY You need to be clearer about what you want out of life. Think about overall goals, then put the necessary changes in place. A bit of self-indulgence won't do any harm, and you could do with some extra spoiling. Emotional affairs suffer under a planetary aspect this evening, and a nostalgic mood might even depress you, but things will go well in the days to come and will restore your faith in life.

14 SUNDAY Plans for the future may well be on your mind, and you are likely to be in an idealistic mood. Plan on: the stars will add the coping stones as you build bridges. Friends are important to you during this phase, and will lighten a sombre mood that may have descended. Things get better very soon, and this evening there's a promise of romance.

15 MONDAY Today the Sun will be lining up with Uranus, so there's an unexpected and rather exciting feel about the day. Anything which comes completely by surprise should be seriously considered, no matter how ridiculous it may seem initially. Always remember that eccentricity is close to genius.

16 TUESDAY Today is the day of the new Moon, and it occurs in the airy sign of Libra. This is an excellent day for taking any kind of short trip or for taking part in a test. A good time, too, for finding bargains around the shops, but only take a smallish amount of money out with you, because you may be a little bit too extravagant if you get carried away.

17 WEDNESDAY Venus has moved into Libra, the area of your chart devoted to the home, so it looks as if you'll be spending a good deal more time there, perhaps doing some decorating or other improvements. The atmosphere between yourself and people you live with should be improving in leaps and bounds. There seems to be a cosy feel where this side to life is concerned.

18 THURSDAY Today Neptune resumes direct movement, so from hereon in matters related to abroad, travelling or further education become a good deal easier to cope with. On a romantic level, you may very well find yourself drawn to someone who comes from abroad, but don't expect this to be the love of your life: just enjoy it for what it is.

19 FRIDAY Relationships at home and at work are in seventh heaven, but Mars could very well put the boot in, so climb down off your soapbox as quickly as you can. It would be a shame to disrupt the more harmonious qualities of life and miss out on a period of uncomplicated enjoyment.

20 SATURDAY As the planets establish a more favourable direction, your day-to-day situation is likely to improve in some way. You may not be offered promotion, but the general circumstances will suit you better. Your practical mood helps you to make a decision if you are faced with a dilemma. Venus right now triggers some exhilarating ideas, some of which may have financial potential.

21 SUNDAY Never underrate your achievements. You may not have reached the giddy heights of success just yet, but you are well on the way. Those of you who take a less humble stance should watch out for arrogance during this phase. Either way, you'll be working hard and could do with a sociable break during the coming weeks: your friends are beginning to wonder if they've offended you.

22 MONDAY You have heard everybody else's opinions on your own business. Now it is time to show that you have your own ideas and to put them into action. This could start a chain reaction of events that will make this day a memorable one. A new romance is likely and for those who are unattached it could bring lasting joy. For those who are not, it will mean hassle and a difficult choice.

23 TUESDAY Today Mercury resumes direct movement, which is good news, because from hereon in you need not fear travelling from place to place, nor taking examinations or tests, nor starting anything new. To your delight, you will find that such matters begin to run a good deal more smoothly, and this gives you the confidence you need if you are to do well.

24 WEDNESDAY Today the Sun will be moving into Scorpio, and that is the area of your chart devoted to fun, sports, children and casual romance. Just make sure that you can tell the difference between an infatuation, a sexual attraction and the real thing, otherwise you could get hurt. However, if you can get into a light-hearted frame of mind and be ready to take advantage of everything and everyone that comes your way, this could be a fun period.

25 THURSDAY Today Mercury is lining up with Saturn, and so you have added concentration to channel into any intricate task or situation. An older person may have an interesting message for you, perhaps when you get home this evening. All in all, this is a good, constructive time, and it could be fantastic on the romantic front.

26 FRIDAY Don't dither. Stick with a plan, and see it through. Your efforts will be rewarded. You could be missing an old friend who has returned home after being with you for a while. A letter brings good news, and a financial burden may now be lifted. Tempers could be frayed at work due to clashes of personality and the unfair treatment of a colleague. You will make a stand and win approval.

27 SATURDAY You'll be delighted at how someone close to you is able to gather their wits about them and sort out

a crisis. This spares you the hassle and enables you to
concentrate on your own problems, which are numerous
enough. Some unexpected news makes it necessary for
you to drop everything and embark on a considerable
journey. The future at work is looking great.

28 SUNDAY Today Mars will be moving into the airy sign
of Aquarius. That is a part of your chart which governs
those you are financially dependent upon, such as your
partner or your boss. Such people may be under some
strain, so if you can think of little ways of making their
load lighter, then you'll be storing up a great deal of
goodwill for the future.

29 MONDAY This is going to be an eventful time and one
that'll start the ball rolling. You'll be invited here and
there and will have difficulty in fitting everything in. A
family celebration – perhaps because of a pregnancy or
wedding – seems likely, and a new job is also on the
cards. All this could put a strain on your finances, and
you must resist the temptation to overspend.

30 TUESDAY The changes that you have been waiting for
have now come about, and something that has always
been just out of reach is finally within your grasp. You
will have to summon up all your courage if a great opportunity and adventure is not to be missed. Don't allow the
chance to slip away. Extra studies connected with your
work could lead to promotion and a decent rise.

31 WEDNESDAY Unfortunately the month ends on a
rather difficult note because of a bad aspect between

Saturn and Pluto. One planet demands change, while the other wants to maintain the status quo. You could run around in circles and so could other people. The best thing to do is to shelve any important decisions until next month if possible.

NOVEMBER

THIS MONTH THE SUN will be swimming along in the watery sign of Scorpio up until the 22nd, and that is the area of your chart devoted to children, creativity, fun and romance. Any decisions or moves you want to make in these areas should be made as soon as possible, preferably on a day which is indicated as lucky in the *Daily Guides*.

On the 23rd, the Sun will be moving into the fiery sign of Sagittarius, so you begin a period in the year when it is necessary to get your head down and do a lot of good work, even though you may find it tedious or boring. Possibly you have left some projects aside in favour of others, and now you are called to turn your attention to them.

November is also an excellent period for visiting the doctor for a checkup if you suspect there's anything wrong; the dentist will be glad to see you too, although no doubt this idea will fill you with trepidation.

Mercury will be in the water sign of Scorpio from the 8th onwards. This is the part of your chart devoted to children, socializing and casual romance, and minor changes are likely in all these areas. If you are creative and are asked to go on a trip or sign an important document, then this is just the time for doing that, because it will be storing up a great deal of goodwill for the very near future.

Venus, too, will be moving into watery Scorpio on the 10th, which is good news, because it throws a happy glow over matters related to children, your social life and romance. It looks as if you're going to be very light-hearted, positive, and full of the joys of living this month.

Fiery Mars will be situated in Aquarius for the entire month. This is the area of your chart devoted to people you are financially dependent upon, both at home or at work, and they may be going through a rather stressful period. See what you can do to be of comfort to them; maybe you can come up with some good ideas on how they can cut down and cope more efficiently. If you can do this, you'll be gaining a lot of prestige.

The pattern the stars make this month suggests that there'll be an inclination for you to start many things, but you may not finish them as efficiently as you should. This must be avoided, so don't turn your attention to anything if you suspect that you may not be able to come through for other people. To do so will lower your credibility, and that, of course, would make you extremely unhappy.

Now look at the *Daily Guides* for further information.

1   **THURSDAY** Today is the day of the full Moon, and it occurs in the earthy sign of Taurus. That is the area of your chart devoted to friends and contacts, and you may find that somebody lets you down, or perhaps someone may be grumpy and difficult to deal with. Use your time for putting the finishing touches to things; in that way you'll be keeping your head down and will therefore be missing some of the flak.

2   FRIDAY Jupiter and Saturn have now moved into retrograde action, and because these planets tend to rule work and career matters, you may find yourself in for a frustrating time. Luckily, you have infinite patience and tenacity when you've really decided what and who you want, and you are certainly going to need those qualities during this period.

3   SATURDAY You have tried to keep everyone happy for long enough. It is time now for you to delegate some of the responsibility to those who have more time to spare than you do. If you are owed some holidays at work, take a few days off. Get away somewhere cosy and relaxing. Moneywise, you are entering a better phase and will be able to splash out on a few luxuries without losing sleep.

4   SUNDAY It has been a busy time for all members of your sign, and your routine has been changed dramatically, but also to your advantage. The changes will continue for a while longer, and there's financial luck and even a touch of romance on the cards. Your health is much improved following a reduction in the stress you have coped with. A phone call from abroad brings news of a reunion.

5   MONDAY There are choices ahead and decisions to be made. Simplify the situation by following your intuition. If you have a hunch about something, follow it. You won't be unhappy at the outcome. There'll be lots of dashing around in the car as you try to catch up on all the visiting of friends that you have neglected for so long. It will pay to discuss finances with a professional.

6   TUESDAY Today the Sun is lining up with Saturn, and because of this those closest to you, both at work and at home, are at their most confident and perhaps a bit too pushy. Never mind, you can't get your own way all the time, and now it is the turn of other people to step into the spotlight. See what you can do to offer backing, advice and encouragement.

7   WEDNESDAY Today the Sun is lining up with Pluto, so you cannot expect things to run as smoothly as you might like. Nevertheless, there is an up side to the day, because it looks as if plenty of invitations for fun and romance are headed in your direction. It's quite likely that someone in your circle might be a little bit jealous.

8   THURSDAY Today Mercury will be moving into Scorpio, so if you happen to be a parent there's a lively feel about your day. For others there may be an inclination to be drawn to something which is intellectually challenging: if so, grab the opportunity with both hands and enjoy it.

9   FRIDAY Venus is about to move into Scorpio, where it will be throwing a rosy glow over matters related to children, social life and casual romance. This is likely to be a thoroughly enjoyable time, but you mustn't take the promises of other people too seriously, because you

know how easily you are hurt. Be casual, and just wait
and see how things develop.

10 SATURDAY You may well look back on this day as a
time when your life changed dramatically. A certain
situation will face you in which you will need to think
fast and make snap decisions. Don't hesitate: your gut
reaction will serve you well. A job you have been
putting off for ages now needs tackling. You may not
enjoy DIY, but eventually it has to be done. A friend
needs your help.

11 SUNDAY You are in one of your spending moods, and
nothing and no-one is going to stop you. Whether it's
new clothes, furniture, or even something major like a
car, you are the sort who simply has to have what your
heart settles on. Luckily, your financial luck is in, and
you will cope with all the expenditure. A phone call
brings news connected with work, and you may have to
go on a journey.

12 MONDAY This should be an eventful and interesting
phase, and for some lucky Cancerians a cash windfall
will pay the way. Discussions concerning a move,
perhaps very soon, are likely to occupy your
thoughts for a while. Legal matters and some extra
paperwork will test your patience, but there can be no
short cuts. Romance may not be on your mind now,
but this could change.

13 TUESDAY No matter how carefully you plan events,
there's always the chance that others will let you

down. Your patience will be stretched to the limit by the sloppy attitude of someone in your circle. But there's a good chance that an escape route out of your frustration may suddenly present itself. Take it. You'll find the change healing and much to your benefit in a more practical way.

14 WEDNESDAY People at home and at work all seem to want your attention, and usually you're happy to cater to everyone's needs, but this time you may have to say 'no'. It seems that one chapter of your life is coming to an end, and you need to spend some time on your own to think. These reflections will influence decisions of a personal and professional nature. What's difficult is that certain people insist on answers now, and you just don't have them. You rarely disappoint, but put yourself first and take the time you need.

15 THURSDAY Today is the day of the new Moon, and it falls in the watery sign of Scorpio. Consequently, there could be a minor new cycle beginning in matters related to children or your social life. Perhaps you've entered a new circle and one member of it is introducing you to a new spare-time activity. Any way you look at this particular day, you're going to be in high spirits and ready to take on board whatever life decides to throw at you.

16 FRIDAY Today Mercury is lining up with Mars, which could make you rather impulsive. This needs conscious controlling, especially when at work, where paperwork could get into a muddle if you are too hasty. This evening it would be a good idea to rest, as you're fast running out of energy.

17 SATURDAY Mercury is lining up with Pluto, so you may change your mind on several important matters a couple of times during this 24-hour period. No doubt this will confuse other people, but on no account should you allow yourself to be pushed or shoved.

18 SUNDAY Today Venus is lining up with Pluto too, so there seem to be some exciting invitations coming your way. If you are a parent, you can make decisions on behalf of your children in the full knowledge that you're going in the right direction. If you're single, keep a high profile this evening, because romance is in the air.

19 MONDAY Your mind will be working overtime today. In some situations analysis is a good idea, but in others, perhaps because you're unable to do anything about matters, it only increases your frustration. Save your fire for a couple of days more; only then will your position be clear. You can be sure of help from workmates, friends or lovers.

20 TUESDAY Venus will once again be lining up with Pluto today, and as a result there may be some changes in connection with property or home affairs. If you are expecting guests this evening, do get on the phone and double-check with them; either they may have forgotten, or perhaps there have been crossed wires in some way.

21 WEDNESDAY The stars suggest a fresh start, so you no longer need to continue with those who question you. Very soon you will realize there are far more appealing alternatives. The choices you face are quite overwhelming, but you feel you must choose soon. However, don't make any decisions just yet, because events over the next few days will make some of them for you, but practical or even health considerations are likely to swing the final vote.

22 THURSDAY The stars indicate a turning point in partnership matters where your input is essential, and with certain other affairs your advice will also be welcome. It's equally important that you make your priorities clear at work or in matters that involve your daily routine, because decisions made today are likely to have far-reaching consequences.

23 FRIDAY Today the Sun will be moving into the fire sign of Sagittarius, and that is the area of your chart devoted to sheer hard work and health matters. Therefore, if you are feeling under the weather, bear in mind that the festive period is not too far ahead, and it might be a good idea to get a checkup or perhaps go on a course of vitamins.

24 SATURDAY Today Venus and Mars are in a difficult aspect. This suggests that mistakes could be made at work, so it might be a good idea to really apply yourself. If you find that concentration is elusive then save important moves till a better day.

25 SUNDAY Today the stars will be opening up the lines of communication between yourself and someone you are financially dependent on. It's time to push aside differences and to reach happy compromises which will satisfy everyone. There's no point in trying to be too independent, because during this time you must listen to other people: if you do, you'll learn a great deal.

26 MONDAY Today Venus is in a difficult aspect with Uranus, and because of this you need to be extremely careful when dealing with those at home. People will be touchy and easily hurt, but as you sometimes suffer from the same problem, you should be able to empathize. This is not a good time for entertaining at home, as things could go wrong.

27 TUESDAY Today Mercury will be moving into the fiery sign of Sagittarius, and that's the area of your chart which rules people you are financially dependent upon. It's likely that your boss or your partner may be signing a contract or perhaps going on a business trip. Either may make you feel a bit neglected, but this is for their own good, so try to be as supportive as you can. You know that if the tables were turned they would certainly be on your side.

28 WEDNESDAY Pay attention to the self-protective instincts you are experiencing. Some may be personal, while others are connected with the family or domestic security. Whichever applies, make your demands with firmness and clarity. Some situations ask for a kind of emotional vulnerability which you find challenging, and they would seem to suggest that your relationship with loved ones is reaching a turning point. Deny your independent streak and show your feelings, no matter how uncomfortable this makes you feel.

29 THURSDAY You may still be hoping that other people realize how difficult their attitude is making situations, but you must accept the fact that a confrontation is necessary. At home, open discussions will allow everyone to make a fresh beginning. You'll just have to hope that differences at work, or those involving legal matters, will improve of their own accord.

30 FRIDAY Today is the day of the full Moon, and it occurs in the airy sign of Gemini, a rather sensitive area of your chart. It's quite likely therefore that your insecurities may be surfacing at this time, and you may be feeling out of sorts with yourself and other people too. The best thing to do is to avoid anything important. Stick to routine, and treat yourself this evening: that will lift your spirits.

DECEMBER

DURING DECEMBER the Sun will be drifting along in the fiery sign of Sagittarius up until the 21st. This is the part of your chart devoted to sheer hard slog, everyday routine and, to some extent, health matters. It might be a good idea to visit your dentist or doctor before the festive period starts, because in that way you can ensure that you're in fine fettle for when all the frivolities start.

On the 22nd, the Sun will be moving into Capricorn. That, of course, is your opposite sign, highlighting your partnerships, both professional and personal. You have a strong need to have attention and to share with other people, and luckily those concerned seem to be like-minded. There's a new closeness building up between yourself and other people; make sure that it lasts well beyond the end of the year.

Mercury will be in Sagittarius up until the 15th; therefore, there's a chance of a new contract being signed in connection with work, or perhaps you will receive an opportunity to go on a trip where professional matters are concerned. However, your energy may be running out at an alarming rate, so it's important that you get in one or two early nights in order that you may get through without too many difficulties.

On the 16th Mercury will be moving into your opposite sign of Capricorn, bringing new faces into your romantic life and perhaps new friends. People you are close to may be feeling restless, and because of this they may plan some kind of trip, perhaps for next year. You may think they're being extravagant, but indulge them: after all, they do indulge you from time to time, you've got to admit.

Venus will be entering Sagittarius on the 3rd. Bearing in mind the time of the year, it's quite clear that there will be social invitations for you to accept in connection with your job. All very well and good, but the temptation to flirt with a colleague in what you believe to be a harmless way could turn into a rather difficult situation. By all means be friendly, and happy-go-lucky, but don't get yourself emotionally entangled.

Mars this month will be moving into Pisces on the 9th,

and after this date it could perhaps be a mistake to travel too far. Those of you who have booked a holiday during the festive period need to double-check all arrangements in order to sidestep any unexpected stress which could crop up. Those who are staying at home can expect a hectic time during the run-up to Christmas, but when it finally arrives you will decide – as you always do – that the effort was well worthwhile.

The pattern the stars make this month is a bit scattered, so there's a suggestion here that you really must concentrate your energies and emotions more than usual; failure to do so will lead other people to believe that you are nothing short of a fly-by-night. If there's one thing you hate, it's finding that people are either humouring you or not taking you seriously, and whether they do so or not depends entirely upon your approach to life this month.

Now look at the *Daily Guides* for further information.

1 SATURDAY Other people, whether at home or at work, appear to be in an aggressive mood, so much so that your instinct is to stand your ground. However, this is one time when you shouldn't act on your gut feeling, because no matter how things appear at this time, other's efforts will eventually be to your best interests, and soon you will find they are only too willing to open some important doors for you.

2 SUNDAY There's a strong possibility that much has happened to you recently, most of which you would prefer to forget. Intense and upsetting as the tensions between you and those closest to you are just now, avoid keeping your thoughts and feelings to yourself, and remember that the only way to solve difficulties is for someone to develop sufficient courage to start talking: let it be you.

3   MONDAY Today the Sun is lining up with Mercury, a clear indication if ever there was one that you are out and about spending your money. Luckily, you're able to find bargains and won't get too carried away. This evening you should keep a high profile and stay on the move: the more activity you cram into your waking hours, the more fun you are likely to find, and perhaps romance may even cross your path.

4   TUESDAY Venus has moved into Sagittarius, and that's the area of your chart devoted to work. If you are at all artistic, or work in a professional partnership, you'll be doing very well until the end of the year. Many of you will need to take care though when attending office parties, because you're going to be at your most flirty, and don't imagine for one moment that your partner won't find out in perhaps the most embarrassing way.

5   WEDNESDAY For one reason or another this seems to be a very special time for you, so don't let minor disagreements or certain people who seem, on the surface anyway, determined to be disagreeable keep you from enjoying it. Remember that those who are being difficult are only trying to tell you, admittedly rather awkwardly, how they feel you can improve your relationships, so listen to them.

6 **THURSDAY** Today Mercury is cosying up to Pluto, which suggests that you will be prone to changes of heart and maybe of mind too. Routine is likely to be interrupted, so be flexible. Also, be prepared for anything that hits you quite suddenly: it could make the difference between success and failure.

7 **FRIDAY** Today the Sun is lining up with Pluto; therefore, it's a day when there's a certain amount of change and frustration, or when a door refuses to open for you. Perhaps you should ease up on your efforts, bearing in mind it is the end of the year: save all your ambitious moves until the festive period is well and truly over.

8 **SATURDAY** Unless you think on your feet and act with the speed of light, situations at work or of a cash nature could get completely out of hand. Initially, these developments may look as if they will be in your favour, but you must be vigilant and keep on top of things, otherwise you run the risk that others may turn them to their own advantage.

9 **SUNDAY** Today Mars will be entering the watery sign of Pisces, the area of your chart devoted to matters related to abroad. Therefore, when travelling, be adaptable and open-minded to the way other people do things. To try to force them around to your way of thinking would be a big mistake. Try to get an early night this evening, as it's likely that your mental energy will be running at a very low ebb at that time.

10 MONDAY Mercury is lining up with Uranus, and this is livening up your emotions. If you're attending office parties, you'll easily be influenced into behaviour that you will feel embarrassed about at a later date. Self-control must be maintained, otherwise it might have been better if you'd simply ignored the invitations, and that would be a shame.

11 TUESDAY It looks as if it's going to be a day when you're confronted with situations in which your timing and your sense of balance are just as important as anything you say or do. In fact, since your intuitions may be less trustworthy than usual, it would be wise to think twice, or even three times, before you act.

12 WEDNESDAY It may appear to you that others are muscling in on plans or decisions that really should be yours to make. However, it might be a good idea to think twice before raising too many objections. Their attitude may leave a little to be desired, but their intentions are good; besides, the people they know and the ideas they introduce could more than compensate for their abruptness or interference.

13 THURSDAY Today Venus is lining up with Jupiter. There is an indication here that you could overindulge or go way over the top. Therefore, if you're attending any kind of social occasion, make sure that you know exactly how you're going to get home. Don't drive if you have been drinking: to do so would be to create unnecessary problems at an important time of the year, which would be a pity.

14 FRIDAY Today is the day of the new Moon, and it occurs in the fiery sign of Sagittarius. New Moons always put you in tip-top shape, and, of course, you're at your most attractive too. This is an excellent time for making a new beginning in any area that you choose, so make this a day when you please yourself.

15 SATURDAY Today Venus is lining up with Pluto, so there could be a certain amount of upheaval and change at home. Maybe people at home are making heavy weather of the festive arrangements, and it needs your imagination to help them to calm down and to get life back into perspective once more.

16 SUNDAY Today Mercury will be moving into Capricorn, and that is your opposite sign. Consequently, new people will be entering your life, perhaps whilst you're out socializing. Where existing relationships are concerned, there's likely to be a certain amount of movement and change, but nothing that you cannot easily cope with.

17 MONDAY Invariably you dash through life without noticing what's going on around you, but now it might be a good idea to slow down and soak up your surroundings. When you do, it would be useful to ask yourself if you're entirely happy or comfortable with what you feel, see or have to live with.

18 TUESDAY Your mind is certainly energized with power and confidence, so if you need to promote and publicize your own personal attributes, you've got a great day for doing just that. Furthermore, you're brimming with positive thinking right now, so, instead of seeing the dark side of life, you now believe in yourself and your talents even more.

19 WEDNESDAY Today Mars will be lining up with Neptune, and this will be energizing your mind, giving you increased imagination but perhaps less patience. If you work in a creative job, take things a step at a time, and don't allow anybody to put unnecessary pressure on you, otherwise you'll finish up exhausted.

20 THURSDAY Anything related to home and those who live there should be put on hold for the time being. It looks as if your emotions are partially or even totally out of sync with the rest of the world, and you lack sufficient mental energy even to consider what needs to be done to reduce the problems of others. There's a possibility that you may be whipping up feelings even more by being vocal about what you see as an injustice.

21 FRIDAY No-one is more interested than you when exciting things happen to people you know or in the world at large, but when it comes to changes in your own life, you can be almost immovable. And yet what has happened is not only intriguing, but worth making an exception for, since it will benefit you greatly in the very near future.

22 SATURDAY Today Mercury will be lining up with Saturn, and because of this the people who are closest to you, both at work and at home, will be changeable, lively, and very amusing. For some there may be a new relationship, but don't tell yourself that this is going to be the love of your life, because if you do I'm afraid you'll finish up hurt, and you don't want that during the festive period.

23 SUNDAY The Sun has now moved into your opposite sign of Capricorn, where it will stay for several weeks. During this time, it is important that you put other people's needs before your own. This is because they are likely to know what is best all round, whereas your own judgement is coloured by an overactive imagination. Problems in relationships can be solved by a sensible talk.

24 MONDAY Delightful opportunities seem to be in the air, but no matter how bewitching they may appear, you would certainly be wise to consider them only as so much talk until you know about another's financial background and stability.

25 TUESDAY Merry Christmas! Today the Moon will be in Aries, so you may not be altogether happy to spend too much time at home. Naturally, you don't want to hurt the feelings of other people, so the best thing to do is to get out into the fresh air for an hour or so: then you can return revitalized and ready to pitch in.

26 WEDNESDAY Because the Moon is in Taurus today, it would be a good idea to spend at least part of the day in the company of friends; you can exchange news and perhaps compare social arrangements for the remainder of the year. You may find you've been invited to the same occasions, in which case you'll be positively delighted.

27 THURSDAY Today Venus will be moving into Capricorn, which is rather a nice aspect, because it puts a happy glow over your existing relationships. Furthermore, if you are fancy-free, then chances to meet interesting members of the opposite sex will be increasing over the next few days.

28 FRIDAY Being disillusioned or let down by those you had thought you could trust is never easy to accept, but strangely, over the next few days or so, you are likely to be thankful for what has occurred. At least now that you know exactly where others stand, you also know in what matters and areas they can be trusted. This is very much a day when adversity can be turned into a blessing.

29 SATURDAY Today the Sun is lining up with Neptune; therefore, it would be a good idea for you to double-check all your social arrangements, as there seems to be a good deal of confusion and muddle around. Furthermore, do make sure that you are not tricked into spending more money than you can cheerfully afford. It's not the amount of money you spend, but who you are spending time with that really makes for a successful evening.

30 SUNDAY Today is the day of the full Moon, and it occurs in your own sign. It looks as if the festivities of the last few weeks are beginning to take their toll, and you're feeling completely exhausted. If you've anything special arranged for tomorrow, it might be a good idea to rest up completely today, so that you are ready to throw yourself into the fray.

31 MONDAY Today Mars is in a difficult aspect with Pluto, which isn't altogether a satisfactory aspect for New Year's Eve. The best thing you can do is to make sure where you're supposed to be, at what time and with whom. Furthermore, avoid the pitfall of using this evening as an excuse to get completely legless: if you do, you won't be pleasing those who mean the most to you, and you don't want to end the year out of favour.

Happy New Year!

DIY ASTROLOGY
Lyn Birkbeck

Do It Yourself Astrology is the first book to bring together in one comprehensive source all the information you need with virtually no calculations to be made. Thorough, fascinating and, above all, easy to use, it includes:

- Tables showing in which Sign of the Zodiac lie your own Sun and Moon, as well as the inner planets Mercury, Venus, Mars, Jupiter and Saturn

- Your personality assessment 'transformer' flow charts show how to resolve problems created by negative character traits and thereby develop the positive ones

- Revealing insights into the seven planetary dimensions of your being and your relationships

- How the outer planets Uranus, Neptune and Pluto the powers of evolution describe your part in the greater scheme of things

- Your Rising Sign your window on the world, and the world's window on you

- Introductions to the Houses, Aspects and compatibility

246 x 189 mm, black & white illustrations and charts
392 pages   ISBN: 1 86204 892 3
£12.99 paperback

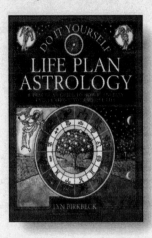

TO ORDER

TITLE	ISBN	PRICE	QUANITY	TOTAL PRICE
				TOTAL

ELEMENT